Graduating College Debt-Free

Skills and Strategies

by Nicole Delorio

Graduating College Debt-Free: Skills and Strategies

Copyright © 2017 Atlantic Publishing Group, Inc.
1405 SW 6th Avenue • Ocala, Florida 34471 • Phone 800-814-1132 • Fax 352-622-1875
Website: www.atlantic-pub.com • Email: sales@atlantic-pub.com
SAN Number: 268-1250

Library of Congress Cataloging-in-Publication Data

Names: Delorio, Nicole, author.
Title: The young adult's guide to graduating college debt-free : skills and strategies / Nicole Delorio.
Description: Ocala, Florida : Atlantic Publishing Group, Inc., 2017.
Identifiers: LCCN 2017035031 (print) | LCCN 2017045021 (ebook) | ISBN 9781620231944 (ebook) | ISBN 9781620231937 (alk. paper) | ISBN 1620231859 (alk. paper)
Subjects: LCSH: College costs--United States. | College students--United States--Finance, Personal. | Student aid--United States. | Education, Higher--United States--Finance.
Classification: LCC LB2342 (ebook) | LCC LB2342 .D456 2017 (print) | DDC 378.3/8--dc23
LC record available at https://lccn.loc.gov/2017035031

Printed in the United States

PROJECT MANAGER AND EDITOR: Danielle Lieneman • dlieneman@atlantic-pub.com
ASSISTANT EDITOR: Lisa McGinnes • lisa@lisamcginnes.com
COVER & JACKET DESIGN: Nicole Sturk • nicolejonessturk@gmail.com
INTERIOR LAYOUT: Antoinette D'Amore • addesign@videotron.ca

Printed on Recycled Paper

Reduce. Reuse.
RECYCLE.

A decade ago, Atlantic Publishing signed the Green Press Initiative. These guidelines promote environmentally friendly practices, such as using recycled stock and vegetable-based inks, avoiding waste, choosing energy-efficient resources, and promoting a no-pulping policy. We now use 100-percent recycled stock on all our books. The results: in one year, switching to post-consumer recycled stock saved 24 mature trees, 5,000 gallons of water, the equivalent of the total energy used for one home in a year, and the equivalent of the greenhouse gases from one car driven for a year.

Over the years, we have adopted a number of dogs from rescues and shelters. First there was Bear and after he passed, Ginger and Scout. Now, we have Kira, another rescue. They have brought immense joy and love not just into our lives, but into the lives of all who met them.

We want you to know a portion of the profits of this book will be donated in Bear, Ginger and Scout's memory to local animal shelters, parks, conservation organizations, and other individuals and nonprofit organizations in need of assistance.

– Douglas & Sherri Brown,
President & Vice-President of Atlantic Publishing

Table of Contents

Chapter 2
Paper, Paper, Everywhere, Nor Any Drop of Ink

CHAPTER 3
The Sea of Scholarships

Chapter 8
Loans as a Last Resort... **135**

Introduction

ongratulations! You're taking the next step in your education to build a successful life. *Graduating College Debt-Free: Skills and Strategies* is one of the most comprehensive books on the market – from providing you with information on loans and scholarships, to budgeting conscientiously, to maintaining good grades, and living smart. Plus, this book gives you unique ideas to save money.

This book is a wealth of knowledge! Your best bet is to read this book cover-to-cover to get the maximum value out of it. If you are short on time or just need to read a chapter on specific content, you can skip to the chapter that you are most interested in. This book holds the key to understanding how much your education costs, how you will foot the tuition bill, and even what types of scholarships and grants can help get you to graduation day without student loan debt.

In Chapter 1, you learn about the effects of having a college degree and how it can save you more money over the course of your life. The chapter also covers why you should save for college while in high school, what you should do to prepare during your time in high school, and how to find your perfect college major.

You can look at why it pays to keep your grades up in Chapter 2. Colleges may never meet with you until after you've stepped onto their campus to take your first class. That's why having good grades, high scores on the SAT or ACT, CLEPing out of college classes, and a wide variety of extracurricular activities shows off your well-roundedness.

Scholarships of wide varieties – based on ethnicity, merit, need, institution, community service, and essays – exist for your use. Chapter 3 gives you the secrets to finding the best scholarships, and what you'll need to stand out from the pack!

In Chapter 4, you will learn about the scholarship application process. You will find a wealth of information in this chapter regarding deadlines, fees, letters of recommendation, essays, and even owning the scholarship interview. The goal is to get you to graduation without a hefty sum of student loans!

You will learn in Chapter 5 about the most powerful tool a student has – financial aid! The Free Application for Federal Student Aid (FAFSA) offers students free money for their education that doesn't need to be repaid! Learn about what you can do to qualify in this chapter.

In Chapter 6, saving money and living cheap is what college is all about. Learn tips and tricks for making the best financial decisions while working toward your college degree. Does the college offer scholarships or grants? What is the cost of public transportation? How much does a class cost? Why does the location of the campus matter to you? Find out in this section!

You will learn the pros and cons about working while in college in Chapter 7. Does your job effect your financial aid? Can your talent as a writer help put you through college? Can working at the Red Cross help your education? Do internships help or hinder your time in college?

In Chapter 8, you'll find out the definition of a student loan and what types of loans are available to you. When do you start paying the money back? How do you get a student loan? Who gives you the borrowed money? You will also learn about the danger of interest and the beauty of payment plans. One can't exist without the other, so fasten your seatbelt while you learn about the wild ride that is interest and how paying off your student loans faster will save you money in the long run.

You will find that graduating debt-free doesn't come without it's challenges in Chapter 9. From credit cards, to loan consolidation, to scholarship scams, to bankruptcy and default – all these situations can cause you to end your college education. By being aware of these dangers, you can successfully get through college debt-free.

Remember, it's always beneficial to read a book cover-to-cover, but if you're short on time, skip through to your favorite chapter. I hope this book provides you will new information on your journey through college, and you are successful at whatever you put your mind to. Best of luck to you in your endeavors!

Chapter 1

How Much Does Education Cost?

ore and more students graduate with debt than ever before. Did you know that your college education at a public institution will cost more than a new Hyundai? That's about $35,000! For that amount, you could purchase a mobile home, a condo, or 56 pairs of Jimmy Choo heels.

According to the National Center for Education Statistics, NCES, going to college has increasingly become more expensive. In 2014-15, the cost skyrocketed to $37,990 — just in time for the next generation to begin their college journey.[1]

---

1. National Center for Education Statistics, 2016

Public colleges boast of their affordability without sacrificing education. In 2014-15, public institutions cost $18,632 for a four-year degree.

That's just for tuition, fees, room and board. The fact is college costs more than the NCES includes in their numbers. You must factor in the cost of food, transportation, and other expenses, especially if you live off campus.

If you're still in high school, do yourself a favor and start researching colleges now! During your junior year, consider researching in-state colleges, the cost of your degree, and where to find scholarships and financial aid. Preparing for college before application deadlines will greatly increase what scholarships and financial aid you receive.

When factoring out the price of college, don't let the cost of tuition make up your mind. With some research, you can find the right college with a price point that you can afford. Not only that, but some colleges offer scholarships based on your extracurricular activities and volunteer hours.

Spend your junior and senior high school years making your background shine! Take part in extracurricular activities. Volunteer at many diverse places. Colleges look for individuals who exceed expectation, and often reward them for their efforts.

Increase Your Power

According to College Board, having a bachelor's degree equips you to earn 60 percent more over the course of a lifetime than if you'd only received a high school diploma.[2] That's a lot of money! The struggles faced when striving for a bachelor's degree are minor when a 60 percent pay increase is at the end of the yellow brick road.

---

2. College Board, 2008.

To increase your power, you must first be knowledgeable about college. If done right, preparing for your future college can be a sanity saving process. Since your workload greatly increases in senior year, it's important to start choosing colleges, completing applications, and submitting financial aid early.

While deciding on a college and major can seem like the biggest hurdle, there are huge decisions to be finalized when it comes to finances – particularly, who will be paying your college tuition.

Making these huge life decisions needs to be a joint effort between you and your parents. Being at odds with your parents during these stressful times can be trying at best. Decide on a peaceable game plan before diving into the college application and scholarship pool.

Remember, the family relationship is changing, and as this process continues, parents want to watch their child emerge into adulthood. Openly communicate with your family about your college desires to get through this stressful time.

Begin the process before your senior year by collecting forms and documents for college admissions, scholarships, and financial aid. The forms include tax returns, financial aid forms, and scholarship applications. This is a great starting point because you can establish priorities before life gets hectic with approaching deadlines. You could oversee seeking admissions and scholarship paperwork, while your parents ensure you keep on track and deadlines are met.

You must be comfortable with your choice of school and major. Since you're living this life, you are the sole person who will live with the consequences of your decisions. However, since fruitful relationships stem from communication, you need to hear your parent's heart. They want what's best for you, and, who knows, they could save you the headache of switching majors down the line with a few wise words! If your parents are contributing financially, it's more than respectful to listen to them. They might have guidelines for what they're willing to pay for.

While you're establishing your independence, it's important to make room for parental involvement. Unless you're emancipated or financially independent from your family, your parents should be involved with the financial aid process. Make this a learning opportunity. Your parents have real world financial knowledge that is invaluable as you grow into adulthood. Learning about how the family finances operate will better prepare you for when you leave the nest.

Making Decisions

It's important to establish a baseline for your college transition. Answering simple questions before graduating high school will save you a major headache:

- **Where are you going to college?** Research in-state versus out-of-state university costs, as well as the cost per credit hour. Private universities boast a better education, but this comes with a hefty price tag. Public or community colleges come with a cheaper price tag, but, in rare cases, without the educational quality offered by others. Keep these ideas in mind when searching for the right college for you.

- **What's your major?** Oftentimes, students arrive at college not knowing what they want to do with their lives. If you're anything like me, you'll change your major three times before ending up in Creative Writing and working for a major publishing company. Use your time in high school to develop your hobbies and entertain any of your interests. Who knows? Your love for drawing could turn into a career in graphic design, or your love for children could turn into a career as a social worker. Shadowing or interning for various companies of interest can determine if a career is right for you!

- **Who's paying for your college degree?** Decide early on who will be helping you pay for your degree. You might receive money for graduating high school, so considering setting this aside for any college-related finances. There are many options, so the burden doesn't have to be placed on one family member. Apply for scholarships and financial aid, and then decide who will pay for the remaining balance. Consider the option to share the load, or maybe extended family might be excited to help you financially in your college education because you're bettering your life.

- **Should you live at home during college?** This question will be addressed in detail further in the book, but the short answer is that's a decision you should make for yourself. There are many, many factors when choosing to move out or live at home – most of which stem from moving into adulthood: home and auto insurance, food, transportation, utilities, cell phone, and…Murphy's Law. "Anything that can go wrong, will go wrong." If you have the savings to live outside the home while factoring in Murphy's Law for various household appliances, you should be golden!

Fast Fact 🁢🁢🁢🁢🁢🁢🁢🁢🁢🁢🁢🁢🁢🁢🁢🁢🁢🁢🁢🁢🁢🁢🁢🁢🁢🁢🁢🁢🁢🁢🁢🁢🁢🁢🁢🁢🁢🁢

The average cost per credit hour at a college – including private and public – is $594.[3] A major is a particular subject someone specializes in at a college. The difference between public and private college is cost, size, and the number of degrees they offer. Private colleges offer fewer degrees, and have smaller class sizes, but can cost more than a public college.

The Independent Student

Financial aid assumes you, the student, have parental involvement during your college transition. Unfortunately, this isn't the case for everyone. Some students' parents are unable to contribute financially, refuse to help, or aren't in their life anymore. Whatever the case, this adds an extra burden to the college prospect since the financial aid office doesn't view you as an independent student.

To declare yourself an independent student you must be: 24 or older by December 31 of the award year, married by the day you file for financial aid, a military veteran, an orphan or ward of the court, or have a child you provide at least half of support for.

There are less recognized ways to get around the financial aid independence process, but you need to provide your college with unusual cir-

---

3. Kirkham, 2017

cumstances to benefit. If your parents are both in jail, institutionalized, hospitalized, or if they've abandoned you, the college will declare you an independent for financial aid purposes. Be prepared to undertake the massive process of filing for independence though.

To declare yourself an independent before you turn 24, bring forward documentation of your unusual situation and a reliable witness such as a clergy member or social worker. Being an independent means receiving more financial aid, so completing paperwork to document your situation will benefit you. In some situations, colleges refuse to grant this status no matter your documentation, so be prepared that your parents might have to complete the FAFSA anyway.

Fast Fact ▫▫▫▫▫▫▫▫▫▫▫▫▫▫▫▫▫▫▫▫▫▫▫▫▫▫▫▫▫▫▫▫▫▫▫▫▫▫▫

FAFSA is the Free Application for Federal Student Aid. It allows students to apply for federal aid to attend college. Many facts are considered when deciding how much aid will be awarded to you: your parent's taxes, cost of attendance, and your expected family contribution.

Another unusual circumstance, though it does happen, occurs when parents have the money to contribute, but refuse to help. This happens for many reasons, usually due to parents wanting their children to establish independence and work for their education. This puts dependent students in a tough situation since the financial aid office views your parents' income as a contribution to your education even if they don't give you a penny. If this is the case, you will need to figure out another way to pay for your education just as your parents want you to do.

Preparation Is Key

By going to college, you are setting yourself up for success over the long term. A good foundation to college includes a solid game plan. Research your local colleges. College course catalogs contain a wealth of information about potential schools. Keep in mind financial aid requirements and deadlines to stay on top of things.

Consider keeping a notebook on hand for your college transition. Get a calendar to keep track of admissions, scholarships deadlines, and important financial aid dates. The last thing you want to do is miss a financial aid or scholarship opportunity because you turned in an application too late.

Make sure to keep copies of financial aid forms and applications on hand, especially if you've applied for many scholarships. Call the admissions office to make sure important applications arrived on time.

Borrowing money to pay for college should be your last option. Accumulating massive debt by the time you've finished college doesn't set you on the path for success. It sets you up to pay off your debt over many years using the job your expensive degree gave you. Let's look at a few ways to avoid this trap!

You will pay less for an education when attending an in-state university as opposed to studying out-of-state or abroad – as enticing as that sounds. Many states offer merit-based and need-based scholarships for qualified students. It helps to keep your grades up, achieve specific scores on the SAT or ACT exams, and perform community service hours. Check with your local colleges about their scholarship requirements to see if you meet the criteria.

Your high-school counselor or local school district will be able to help you during your junior or senior years to see what programs are available and how you can apply. Depending on the college, you may receive grants or scholarships to help pay for tuition, books, and room and board. Every little scholarship adds up in the long run, so don't be afraid to ask about unclaimed scholarship funds as well. One girl ended up with $8,000 in unclaimed scholarships over her four-year degree because of one email!

Save, Save, Save

Either when you're born or sometime during your childhood, parents may set aside money for your education. Many states have savings plans offering tax benefits that continue well into your college education. Not only does a savings account reduce your financial aid need, it also reduces your need to take out expensive loans.

There is a mistaken belief that savings is going to reduce the amount of financial aid you receive. It is true that if your parents saved enough money to finance your entire education, then you're not going to receive as much financial aid as though you had no savings at all. However, only a portion of savings is counted toward the expected family contribution. It's better to have saved along the way than to have spent the money and hoped for a large financial aid check.

Financial aid doesn't expect parents to put their entire life savings into your education. The process recognizes that families have other expenses and even other children to finance through college.

Tips on how to save money include:

- Not saving money in your name. Have it in your parents' name instead to produce the most interest and tax benefits. The financial aid office counts your savings toward the amount of financial aid you can receive. Your savings is counted as your assets and it is assumed that you will be using this money for your education.

- The best college savings plan comes from consistency and time. If your parents saved $25 a week from the time you were born until you turned 17, at a five percent interest the total would be $34,839. Even if your parents started saving when you were older, any form of savings helps in the long run.

- A simple way to save money would be to place money in a regular savings account at a bank. The downside to this is you are going to earn a low interest rate, and will have to pay federal and state income taxes on what you earn.

- A better way to save for college is a Section 529 plan. Since these plans are administered by the states, the rules vary, but the premise stays the same. The money placed in the account is tax-deferred – a huge benefit – and the bonus is that qualified disbursements are not taxed either. This is a major advantage for you and your parents for saving the most money. For example, if Joe Schmoe's parents invested $500 for his college by putting the money into a Section 529 plan, then, when they take out the money to pay for Joe's education, the money wouldn't be taxed.

• If planned far enough ahead, consider investing in a Section 529 Prepaid Tuition Plan. This plan allows for your parents to lock in an in-state tuition at public schools at current prices. If your parents purchase a half a year's tuition, it will always be worth a half a year's tuition, regardless of how much time has gone by. This plan is only beneficial to you if you attend a public school in your state. On the plus side, prepaid tuition is also counted as a parental asset, meaning you can still qualify for financial aid even if your tuition is completely paid for.[4]

• Also consider the Coverdell Education Savings Account (ESA). These accounts, created under the Taxpayer Relief Act of 1997, allow friends and family to contribute up to $2,000 a year toward your education.[5] These accounts are considered an asset of the owner for financial aid purposes. In most case, the account is in your parents' name, but once you turn 18, the account defers to you. Unless your parents filed the necessary paperwork to keep the account in their name once you turn 18, the account transferring over to you will reduce your financial aid eligibility. Remember, Coverdell accounts are taxable, although withdrawals for higher education purposes are not.

---

4. U.S. Securities And Exchange Commission, 2012
5. Internal Revenue Service, 2016

Should I Get a Job?

You and your parents may be wondering if you should get a job to pay for college. Remember, the money in your personal savings counts as an asset, which decreases your financial aid eligibility. In short, getting a job would hinder your finances.

Any income you earn over $3,000 will count against you and decrease your financial aid. You are better off spending your time volunteering, preparing for college, and taking part in extracurricular activities than working at a job. By preparing this way, you will look good on paper to colleges and, in return, have a greater chance at receiving financial aid and scholarships.

Chapter 2

Paper, Paper, Everywhere, Nor Any Drop of Ink

ooking good on paper increases your chances of receiving financial aid and scholarships – even getting accepted to the college of your dreams! Right now you might be thinking, "Where do I even begin?" Rest assured that the blank college papers in front of you will soon be filled in by your knowledgeable hand!

Look Fantastic on Paper

Part of preparing for college is considering how your record will look to admissions and scholarship committees. The admissions officers and scholarship committees do not know you, therefore, you must look great on paper. The only things they know about you are what courses you've taken, the grades you've earned, and the extracurricular activities and volunteer hours you've done. Since your personality can't be conveyed on paper, you need to show the committee your passion through various activities.

Translate your interests to paper. For example, you may possess the greatest leadership skills in the world, but unless you have held leadership positions in clubs or school government, no one on the committee will ever know. If you're a gifted musician, debater, or chess player, translate these skills into accomplishments outside practicing at home or your talents will go unnoticed, and your chances for scholarships will be small.

Keep this in mind:

- Once again, keep copies of important documents, awards, certificates, and other paperwork that prove that you were awarded what you claim you did. Keep the paperwork in a place you'll remember, like a file cabinet, to use for college fund searching or even when applying for work in the future.

- Whenever you volunteer, get the name, contact information, and signature of those that can prove you did the work you claim. If you volunteered at a local organization, keep the name, address, and phone number of the organization, and the name of your supervisor. This may seem excessive, but it can save you the pain of proving your community service hours later. Your supervisor may be able to help later with a letter of recommendation, or even a future job.

- Network, network, network! You may have been to a career fair, or even heard your parents discussing the importance of networking with other people in different fields. Keeping your contacts up to date even if you no longer work with a club or organization anymore is crucial. It is in your best interest to maintain old relationships with people you might need later. By staying in touch, you are providing yourself with someone that could put you in contact with a potential future employer.

CASE STUDY: Debra Lipphardt

College is more than a dream and you don't have to go into deep debt to make it possible.

However, you do need to be realistic; you may have to attend a local school and live at home a bit longer, or go to a school that offers you more in scholarships, or you may have to take online classes while you work to help defray the costs, but there are also other ways to help, such as scholarships. The more you win in scholarships, the wider your options become.

Jennifer, Carla, Mick, and Daniel, all four above average students, with average test scores, and with no financial need grants (i.e.; Pell) went through four years either 100% debt free, or with minimal costs. They did this by applying for as many scholarships as possible and attending either local schools or the ones that offered them the most money, and there are many many more students just like them.

However, if you are in the top 10%, have great test scores, their is even more money and opportunities out there for you.

Alphonso applied for every scholarship possible. He was extremely smart, a minority student, and had financial need, so when he was accepted into an Ivy League school, much was already covered, as this school doesn't believe in loans. This did not stop him from applying for other scholarships though. He went on to win a national one that covered not only the rest of his costs, but also helped pay for much of his graduate school as well.

Then there is Tim. Tim is also a highly intelligent young man. During his junior and senior year he continuously applied for multiple scholarships and was offered over one million dollars in scholarship money. He earned enough to cover all of his costs (tuition to living) at MIT (and they do believe in loans). Neither one of these young men 'assumed' that everything would be taken care of. They did it themselves, by searching, questioning, and applying for everything that they could possibly could, being humble and thankful for all, that they won.

You not only have to work hard applying for scholarships, but you also need to make smart choices about the school you attend in order to avoid or minimize debts that college can bring, but as in just the few students mentioned, it is definitely doable.

Debra Lipphardt is the author of *The Scholarship & Financial Aid Solution*, a book geared towards finding scholarships and tips on the entire process of applying for them. The book was written to help ease the process of scholarships for both students and parents alike, nationwide. Debra has also recently written some chapters for a textbook on scholarships and career and college choices.

She is the College/Career/Scholarship Coordinator for a high school whose students have averaged over six million dollars yearly in scholarships.

Maintain Your Grades

A good rule of thumb to live by is make sure your Grade Point Average (GPA) stays higher than gas prices. This may not always be valid

– especially in today's economy – but strive for it while the humor is still relevant.

Keeping your GPA up is the most important goal you can achieve in high school. Your GPA is how you will be compared to others, and may even be the basis for how many scholarships you receive. Even a small increase in your GPA can make a difference of thousands of dollars. The safest bet when it comes to scholarship money is to work hard for the best GPA possible.

Good grades are one of the best investments in your future you can make. Some schools hand out full scholarships to students with a certain GPA and SAT/ACT score. Even the schools that do not have full-ride academic scholarships often give a higher percentage of aid to students with high grades. Many schools give out merit scholarships, some regardless of need and some not.

Keeping your grades up for four years of high school requires a commitment on your part, but even if you didn't do so well in your freshman and sophomore years, you can still bring your average up if you work at it. Any increase will be worth the effort. Do not take the easy way out by avoiding challenging courses. It might be easier to make high grades in easy courses, but scholarship committees will take one look at your transcripts and not be impressed.

When choosing your high school courses, follow your high school's college preparatory guidelines. Also, look at what the colleges you are interested in require of incoming freshmen as more colleges are considering the difficulty of your courses when making their decisions. Make sure you have covered all the bases. If you excel in a subject, such as math or history, make the most of it. Take the hardest courses your school offers in that subject and put forth your best effort.

SATs & ACTs

The SAT and ACT are the most important tests you will take in high school. Every year, there are calls for schools to rely less on standardized testing, but the reality is that the SAT and ACT are objective measurements schools can use to compare students from different backgrounds. Colleges require different tests to enroll, so make sure you know your college's enrollment policy.

Most scholarship committees rely heavily on SAT and ACT scores because they're a convenient way of comparing students from different backgrounds. Most scholarships are based on the highest scores and grade point average. Others will review your extracurricular and community service activities as well.

Since colleges use the SATs for admission, it's safe to say that achieving high scores will ensure they choose you for their program. Taking the SAT Subject Test guarantees the College Board will look twice at your application. The SAT Subject Tests are 20 multiple-choice tests given on individual subjects. You can choose which subject you want to test on to achieve a high score.

Every test is one hour long with the option to take up to three SAT Subject Tests in one day. Take advantage of the opportunity! Some colleges require the test for admission, while other recommend taking it since it looks great on an academic resume. The choice is up to you.

An excellent way to improve your chances of getting into the college you want and getting it paid for is to make the best possible score on the SAT and the ACT. Studies have shown that a test preparation course can increase a student's performance immensely, so investing in a prep course may be worth the cost if it helps you get more scholarship money. This can mean thousands of dollars in aid. Choosing to prepare for the upcoming tests can mean the difference of a significant scholarship.

Invest in a reasonably priced preparatory course. If you cannot find a course in your area, there are books available to purchase or borrow from the library.

If you're struggling to pass the SAT or ACT, consider getting a tutor who can offer you one-on-one assistance. Tests are important to pass with as high a score as possible, especially since test scores are designed for college entrance.

Simple tips to pass the SAT or ACT include:

- Prepare for the test. Study the materials.
  Do not wait until the last minute!
- Try not to relax, do not stress, and get a good night's sleep the night before your test.

- Read the test directions carefully.
- Read the questions carefully. If it is a multiple-choice test, look over every possible answer before deciding.
- Answer the questions you know first, and then go over the ones that will take more time.
- Review your responses.
- Double check that you have answered all the questions.
- Pace yourself.
- Answer every question on the ACT and SAT. You have a 20 percent chance of getting it right! So when they announce the final 10-minute call for each section, quickly answer every one of them.

It's a great idea to take the SAT and ACT the second half of your junior year. If the college you are applying to accepts either score, then you can retake the one you did best on if need be. You want your best scores for college application by late fall of your senior year, because many colleges have already accepted students by then.

Extracurricular Activities

Whether you're busy academically or not, there will come a time when you will wish you'd participated in extracurricular activities. They can be difficult to choose! Some academically gifted students would rather concentrate on their studies and feel they don't have time to devote to other things. When it comes time to complete college admissions and scholarships, you will wish you participated in extracurriculars.

Colleges aren't always looking for the best grades. They're looking for the individual with the grades and extracurricular activities to back it up.

A well-rounded student will leave college having real life experience, not just book knowledge.

Since there are many opportunities at school and within the community, finding extracurricular activities isn't difficult. You could invent your own project or get involved in a friend's group. College's look for creativity and leadership, so inventing your own project and inviting classmates looks great on an application.

Should you devote all your time to one activity or get involved in as many activities as possible? The answer lies somewhere in between. You might be interested in only one area, such as sports, writing, or photography. You might be the type of student to try many different activities, but never stick with one long. Or, you might be a combination of the two.

Since scholarships committees and admissions officers are going to look at the range of your activities and the depth of your involvement, it's best to have a mix of many involved activities on your resume. Find an activity you enjoy, and go for mastery. Do many things, but show commitment. Mix it up by becoming a member or officer of a club, playing on a sports team, or doing something to help your community.

Don't forget to look outside of your school as well. School activities aren't the only activities that count. Almost anything you do, including helping at your church, doing ham radio, or founding/participating in a local square-dance club, will count. Volunteer in fields you're interested in. If you enjoy health care, volunteer at a nursing home or local hospital.

If your activities are heavily weighted in one area, do some quick and simple activities to broaden your resume. Since your time is limited during your senior year, look for things in the community or school that will show your well-rounded skills.

Home-Schoolers

The popularity of home school has exploded in recent years! Admissions officials and scholarship committees have become accustomed to making decisions about students with alternative records, which is what they consider home schooling. Home-schooled students also enjoy a reputation as being well prepared for college, and they tend to score better on the SATs and other standardized tests than regular students. Admissions officials are aware of this, but admissions policies vary by state, or even from school to school.

You might find yourself wondering how to apply for scholarships and financial aid if you've been home schooled. You're in luck! Many schools are opening the admissions process to better measure the alternative education that home-schoolers have received.

Talk to the admissions offices of schools you plan to attend by your junior year. Ask them what documentation they are going to require and what you can do to ensure that you will be accepted. Your school may have a policy in place, or they may be willing to work with you on an alternative application. The responsibility is going to be on you.

The big problem you are going to run into is that your mom or dad, or whoever has taught you, has given you grades for courses that only you took. In other words, grades your parents gave you can't be compared with other students, which admissions officers need to judge your worthiness. To put together a convincing application, you need to think about solid ways you can demonstrate your abilities so that they can be compared with others. Keep copies of tests you have taken, essays you have written, and research projects you have completed. This can show that you have learned the same material as public-school students.

Of course, the most important thing you can do is to score well on the SAT/ACT. This is the most solid measurement that admissions and scholarship officials will have to compare you with others. If you can manage a near-perfect score, school officials are not going to care if were schooled at home, in Kathmandu, or under a rock. You are going to get accepted and get financial aid and scholarships based on the scores alone.

You need to make friends with your local school system, because they can provide you with help. The guidance counselor can help when preparing for the SATs or ACTs, and completing other tasks. You should also be able to take part in extracurricular activities like sports, clubs, band, the school newspaper, or academic teams, if you so desire.

If you do find that you are denied access to school activities, then you will need to fill the gap yourself. You have the same opportunity as regular students to exhibit your leadership skills by spearheading community service projects or by finding other ways of demonstrating your leadership ability. You can also join recreational sports teams not related to the schools, and clubs or organizations as well. Your church is also a good place to start. Be sure that you can document these activities and the extent of your participation and leadership.

Advanced Placement and CLEP

A great way to gain college credit while still in high school is through Advanced Placement (AP) courses or College-Level Examination Program (CLEP) exams. You can combine the two to get maximum punch.

AP classes allow you to earn college credit for high school courses that you would take anyway. For example, instead of taking senior English and getting a course credit, take AP English and get the usual course credit plus the opportunity to earn college credit. The AP designation simply means that at the end of the course you can take a standardized exam for college credit.

The College Board administers the AP program and testing. The higher your score, the more credit you earn. At this time, AP exams are offered in 35 different subjects, including various sciences, calculus, statistics, computer science, English, seven different foreign languages, government and other social sciences, music theory, and studio art. Ask your school counselor about which courses are offered at your school and at what times. The cost of an AP exam is about $93, which is a real bargain compared to the cost of tuition.[6] Many schools even cover the cost of the exam, making it free for you!

Be aware that these courses are designed to be taught at a college level, so they are going to move at a faster pace and cover more material than a regular high school class. In other words, do not try to do everything at once during your senior year. Take a couple of AP courses during your junior year and a couple more your senior year.

If you make high scores on the exams, you could be granted a half of a year's worth of college credit, which will cut your college costs by 12 to 25 percent. And you have gained high school credit to boot. Schools usually give you weighted points on the GPA scale for AP classes, so this will boost your overall ranking as well.

The College Board also runs the CLEP program, but it is much broader in scope than the AP. CLEP tests are for anyone, regardless of ages or educational background. Each exam offers between 3 and 12 college credits, which are accepted by more than 2,000 colleges across the country. Again, check with the schools you plan to apply to and ask if they will accept these credits.

Many schools accept CLEP credits only in certain subjects. Each exam costs $85, which, like the AP exam, is a real bargain. Exams are offered

---

6. College Board, 2017

in a much broader range of areas than the AP, including such subjects as accounting, marketing, and human growth and development.

These programs are excellent ways to not only slash your college costs significantly but also help prepare you for college courses, and they are well worth the effort.

Community College Courses

Community colleges, and even four-year schools, are reaching out more than ever to nontraditional students. Courses are offered at branch campuses or online, and many are offered evenings or in the summer.

These are real college courses, so be prepared to devote the time and effort necessary to do a good job and keep up your grades. These will be the cheapest courses you are going to find, but keep in mind that since you are not a full-time student, you are not going to receive much financial aid.

Many schools offer "dual enrollment", which in most places, is free. You take the classes during school hours (or evenings if you prefer), earning both high school and college credits at the same time. Some high schools even offer the college classes on their own campus. Students can go to both high school and college at the same time.

Others can only attend dual enrollment classes during their last year of high school, assuming they have met all the requirements. Keep in mind that time spent working on night or online courses is time spent away from your high school courses or scholarship searches and that college classes will require more work than most high school classes. In other words, do not squander an opportunity to win a big scholarship so that you can knock out a few courses on the cheap.

These courses might work better for you in the summer, when you do not have the burdens of your regular schoolwork. Most schools have liberal admissions policies, so you might be able to take a couple of courses between your junior and senior years, and then a couple more between graduation and your first semester at college.

Another way that community colleges can save you money is the transfer trick. You can complete your first two years at an inexpensive community or junior college and then transfer to the college of your choice to complete your degree. You can save many thousands of dollars this way, especially if you live at home while attending, and you will still end up with the same degree. Many times, living on campus is costlier than the college tuition and fees itself.

Chapter 3

The Sea of Scholarships

Sifting through the multitude of scholarships on the internet, at your school, or even on a bulletin at your local grocer can be overwhelming. Luckily, in this chapter, you'll learn the easiest methods for finding scholarships, creating applications, and watching the money roll in.

First, let's discuss the different types of scholarships up for grabs:

- **Merit-based:** Determined by your ability in sports, academics, or other areas
- **Need-based:** Determined by you and your family's financial situation

- **Ethnicity-based:** Determined by your race, religion, or national origin
- **Institutional-based:** Awarded by some colleges or universities
- **Community Service-based:** Determined by the hours and the dedication to the service you gave
- **Essay-based:** Determined by the creativity of an essay required
- **Other:** Scholarships are awarded for many reasons, sometimes including all the above

Remember, when applying for scholarships:

- You should apply as early as you can — high school is a good time to start, and your senior year is most likely the best year of your life to apply. Not only are there more local scholarships offered than any other time, but your competition is not as fierce as other years.

- The more scholarships that you apply for, the more likely you are to receive one or more.

- Do not assume that because a scholarship is small that it does not count. It all adds up. Even one for only $100 might still pay for a book or two.

- Pay attention to details when filling out all your forms. Make sure everything is right in terms of content and that it has no grammatical errors. You do not want to miss a scholarship because you forgot to include something or used the wrong color ink.

- Everyone can find some kind of scholarship they are qualified to receive.

- Keep looking even after you think you have exhausted your possibilities.

- Do not stop at one. You may be eligible to receive more. Apply, Apply, Apply!

Colleges are always looking for well-rounded individuals to receive funds. They search for unique individuals with leadership qualities to add to their college alumni. With any luck, the student will graduate and move on to change the world, all the while crediting their college with some of their success. That's the hope at least.

How do you make your resume stand out from the pack?

- **Letters of recommendation:** Either from a teacher, an alumnus, an employer, a leader in your church, a prominent member of your community, a coach, or anyone else that can point out your strengths. You also will most likely need one from someone in administration (required by many scholarships). This would include your principal, assistant principal, or guidance counselor. Be sure to give them a resume of all your accomplishments, including academic awards, extracurricular activities (sports, clubs, any organization that you belong to), and community service. Most of these people do not know all that you do, and the resume will help them write a better letter.

- **An essay:** The college essay you write serves the purpose of convincing admission officers that you should be admitted into their school because of what you offer in terms of academic achievements, community service, athletic abilities, and so on. The most common scholarship essay is the one asking about your goals, college and career.

When working on defining yourself and figuring out what kinds of scholarships you might be eligible for, you might want to start with a list of achievements that covers the following: school achievements, school contacts, degrees/certificates, contacts, your interests, memberships, your strengths, your focus on studies, your career focus, your paperwork, and any obstacles you've overcome.

Academics

Academics include your overall GPA during high school. If a student's been dedicated all four years, then he or she will shine through. SAT and/or ACT scores also fall under academics. Most colleges accept scores from either test, but a select few prefer the SAT. These scores are on your transcripts, as long you filled in the required school code on the application. National-level scholarships may also request scores to be sent directly from the test site.

A very common requirement for most applications is an official transcript to validate your grades and test scores. You can usually get these from the guidance counselor's office. Transcripts include all your high school classes and semester/yearly grades, test scores, and sometimes various activities and service hours. Official transcripts come in a sealed envelope and must not be opened. If you do, the transcript will no longer be official.

Awards and Honors

The awards and honors section varies. Some applications want you to list all awards or honors, while others ask specifically for either academic awards and honors or non-academic awards and honors.

Academic awards include your program of study such as honors classes, AP classes, the International Baccalaureate Program, ACE, or dual enrollment. These courses show that you've taken a rigorous curriculum path. Other academic recognitions include class rank or whether the student is graduating with honors, high honors, or highest honors.

Another academic achievement is being a member of the National Honors Society. Even though it also counts as a membership in an organization, it still goes under 'awards' because the student was invited to be a member due to their academic (and in some schools, discipline, too) history.

You should also include any other awards you have won because of your grades. Students need to keep track of every award they receive in high school including classroom awards (i.e. math, science, English) or any faculty-selected awards. If a student is a member of an academic team, this would be considered an academic award, just as attending any summer college programs would also go under this heading. Both entail academic achievements from the student.

Non-academic awards include being a captain of a team, an officer of a club, a member of a varsity team, and any other awards the student may have received from a sport, club, or organization. Another type of non-academic award is a volunteer (or community service) award, which is usually harder to come by, as you need a considerable number of hours to receive this.

Leadership

Leadership skills aren't required for all scholarship applications, yet you will see this section on many of them. Being an officer of a club, a captain on a team or a member of student council or government are obviously leadership positions, but there are other types as well. You might have led a committee, coached a younger team, tutored someone, taken care of younger children, or even directed your co-workers.

These situations show that your leadership skills set an example for others. You could've helped organize a project in one of your classes or led a group who helped make a difference, even a small one. These acts of service display qualities of leadership. Think hard—you've probably applied some form of leadership skills to a situation without even realizing it.

Test Scores

Listing SAT and/or ACT scores is a common requirement on most scholarship applications, but these vary from state to state. In Florida, for example, CPT or PERT tests can substitute for the SAT or ACT, but they are for community college admissions only. Many students prefer to take these exams rather than the SAT or ACT, because they seem easier and are less expensive, but they've never been required on any scholarship application.

These tests are expensive, and most students usually take them more than once. Students from low income-families can use waivers, usually twice per year during their junior and senior years, if they receive free or reduced lunches. They should visit their guidance counselor to see if they qualify.

You do not have to have the highest scores to win certain scholarships because many other factors are considered. Taking the exams shows that students are serious about going to college. However, if the scholarship is based solely on academics or if you are applying for any national academic type scholarships, the higher the scores are the better chances you will have to win.

Extracurricular Activities

Extracurricular activities include recreation before or after school hours and not receiving grades, credit, or payment for participation. They can be school-related or non-school related as well. As long you meet at least once monthly and in an organized manner, you can even count the Butterfly Club as an extracurricular activity. These activities show dedication, commitment, and involvement beyond the required school courses and hours. They also show that you'll grow up to be a productive, caring member of your community.

Joining the school band or ROTC can also count as extracurricular activities if students participate in them after or before school hours. If you get a grade or credit for the activity, it's no longer considered extracurricular. Remember to always list the number of years for any position or office you held. Include any type of awards you received as part of that club or sport, unless you listed that award somewhere else on the application.

Always remember that an extracurricular activity is any type of organization you belong to and that you actively participate in. You do not need to be the leader to be a large factor in your club because a club cannot function without members. Most organizations are also a good way to become involved in community service projects that involve helping others or making your community a better place to live.

Community Service/Volunteering

Community service involves helping a non-profit organization or needy individuals for free. Helping your family does not count, nor can you receive pay for it. Also, community service given by a judge does not count toward community service hours either. Believe it or not, this question is asked every year.

There are numerous ways to receive service hours and many different places that need your help. You can pick and choose the one that is right for you. For example, if you feel that you want to go into the medical field, you could volunteer at a hospital or clinic.

However, if you volunteer at a doctor's office, veterinarian's office, or dentist's office, (which are for-profit organizations) it cannot count towards community service hours.

You can still include it under the "extracurricular" section, but you should state that it was volunteer work, because most scholarship committees will take the hours into consideration. Most importantly, your specified volunteer work shows that you are serious about your career path.

Church is also a great type of community service. You could be part of the choir, be an usher, help with technical work, or maybe teach Sunday school. Helping your church in any way counts for community service hours except, of course, attending church services. Include mission trips (local, out-of-state, or out of the country) as well.

When listing service hours on a scholarship application, make sure to list the hours and the number of years for each activity. If you are an officer, you can keep hours such as organizing and delegating, separate from the actual activity if you wish. Always keep track of the hours you spend as a leader because the number of hours adds up even for just one event. You can also list different projects you worked on separately and not under the club, especially if they required a plethora of hours.

Once again, it's extremely important to keep track of all your hours in any type of community service. Usually, students turn in their hours (signed by someone you worked for) to the guidance counselor or the student activity director, and they record the hours in the computer, so that it's on the student's transcripts. Students should make sure they document all hours, dates and time, and descriptions with the correct number of hours.

Essay-Based Scholarships

There are many scholarships that are based solely on an essay or for which the essay may be a determining factor. Almost all scholarship applications have an essay question, even if it's only a paragraph long. For seniors, these essays usually focus on your personal thoughts and come from the heart, rather than a research report. The most common question is: "What are your education and career goals?" The answer for this can be anywhere from 100 to 500 words, depending on the application.

Some scholarships require an essay only. Anyone can apply for these. They do not require a certain GPA, community service, or extracurricular activities, which is great for many students. Some may involve a little research, but most for seniors at least, are just common sense, opinionated essays.

Most students don't enjoy writing essays, especially prompts that require extra work. If the question makes it necessary for you to read a book or do research for the essay, the competition is cut way down and opens the door for more chances to win.

Financial-Need Scholarships

There are scholarships mainly based on financial need, according to the parents' or guardians' income. Some are based only on income, such as the Pell Grant from FAFSA, while others ask about extenuating circumstances, which can vary. However, extenuating circumstances can be a variety of different situations, such as a change in one of the parents' jobs (unemployment, less hours, or changing to an occupation with less income), separation or divorce, extra medical bills, or maybe a grandparent or another family member recently moved in with you.

Those situations fall under unusual financial circumstances or financial need with circumstances. Perhaps your parents just refuse to help finance any of your college education. Another factor could be that your parents make too much to receive any grants but not enough to pay for your college costs. No matter which category you fall into, you need to notify the scholarship committee about your financial situation.

Scholarships for Minorities

Minority scholarships vary. Some are for individual minorities only, and others for African Americans, Hispanics, Native Indians, and Asians. Just don't wait until your senior year to do this because time might be a factor in receiving your membership. On most minority scholarships, unless specified, you do not have to be 100 percent of that ethnic group to qualify.

Most of these scholarships are found online, but many local ones come from different organizations or even ones for certain majors. There are scholarship applications that are for minorities only because there's a greater need for those types of employees in specific career fields. There are even some for females of any race because the glass ceiling is still there. It's best to put your race on your official transcripts to prove your heritage, even if you are only 1/8 of that ethnicity.

Scholarships for Specific Majors

There are many scholarships based on the student's planned major, even if they haven't firmly decided to stick with that major down the road. The most common essay question is about education and career goals. Even if a student is not completely sure about which major to choose, he or she must have one career choice that interests him or her.

Scholarships that require enrolling in a specific major are usually from companies or organizations that specialize in that field. Jobs may even be offered to scholarship winners upon graduation or as internships.

Most companies will never even see the student, but sometimes they host award ceremonies for the winners. Typically, they don't keep tabs on students who win. So, if this is the case, then changing your major later down the road will not affect your scholarship. However, there are a few scholarships that are renewable while the student is in college, if the major stays the same.

Fast Fact ▪▫▪▫▪▫▪▫▪▫▪▫▪▫▪▫▪▫▪▫▪▫▪▫▪▫▪▫▪▫▪▫▪

In Florida, residents can apply for the Florida Bright Futures Scholarship Program, a program that establishes three lottery-funded scholarships to reward high school graduates for academic achievement. They can apply for other funds, such as the José Martí Scholarship Challenge Grant Fund and receive $2,000 per year. This need-based merit award is designed for eligible students of Hispanic origin who will attend Florida public or eligible private institutions and are enrolled in a minimum of 12 credit hours for undergraduate study or 9 credit hours for graduate study. For more information, contact the Florida Department of Education's Office of Student Financial Assistance at 888-827-2004 or visit **www.floridastudentfinancia aid.org**, or check with your school's financial aid office.d to you: your parent's taxes, cost of attendance, and your expected family contribution.

CASE STUDY:
Yvonne Bertovich

Striving toward a Bright Futures Scholarship was never a question for me, even though my attendance at a state school was. I had the untypically typical dream of going away to college — like really away — to the snow and aging campuses of the Northeast. I did manage to make it north and east, just not by very much. Being raised in Tampa for most of my life, Gainesville and the University of Florida ended up exceeding all of my expectations.

Even though by out-of-state standards UF seemed like a bargain, Bright Futures has easily cut my tuition in half every single semester. I cut costs further with additional scholarships I earned for academics once I became established at UF. Thankfully, my family has been able to use savings as well as my scholarships effectively and we've never taken out any additional loans, even when my dad was between jobs. While in college, I have had up to three paid positions at a time, but I was able to use this money for studying abroad and other fun expenses.

Bright Futures has been beyond worth it when considering what I had to accomplish when I was still in high school — honestly, I wanted to do all of that stuff anyway. I coasted in some classes and busted my butt in others to earn straight As, and, truthfully, I could have studied a bit harder for the math portion of the SAT. The 100+ hours of volunteer work needed to qualify were a bit hard-fought, but dedicating your time to one specific program and knocking it out in chunks is the way to go. I spent roughly three summers throughout high school driving myself (in my own car, thanks Mom and Dad) to an industrial part of Tampa to volunteer at Feeding America a few days a week. It didn't smell great, but, like I said, it was rewarding beyond measure.

I didn't even qualify for the highest award amount of Bright Futures, only the second highest. Perfectionist, high school me is dying inside somewhere that I'm disclosing this to anyone other than my parents.

As a journalism major now, it's no wonder my math SAT scores were 10 points below the cut-off. Of course, my reading and writing scores carried me far beyond where I needed to be. Even though this was hard for me to swallow at the time, when it comes to help paying for school, you learn to be nothing but grateful. There is nothing more valuable than an education and the freedom to learn, and Bright Futures allows some more peace of mind so you can afford that extra latte or two while studying. You're gonna need it.

Yvonne is currently a senior studying journalism at the University of Florida.

Unique or Unusual Scholarships

There are also "unusual" scholarships that everyone talks about. Unfortunately, no one knows what they're called or how to find them. For example, there is a scholarship for left-handed people. Rolex has a scholarship for $25,000 if you can pass their rigorous scuba-diving requirements.[7]

Another scholarship includes the Chick and Sophie Major Memorial Duck Calling Contest. According to Scholarships.com, "The Chick & Sophie Major Memorial Scholarship Duck Calling Contest is open to any high school senior in the United States who can call ducks. During its 38-year history, the renowned contest has awarded more than $60,000 in scholarships to young duck callers attending 32 different colleges and universities in 13 different states." The scholarship awards $2,000 to the best duck caller.[8]

The Van Valkenburg Memorial Scholarship offers a $1,000 scholarship to those who can prove their relation to Lambert and Annetje Van Valkenburg through birth or legal adoption. According to navvf.

7. Scholarships, 2017
8. Stuttgart Kansas, 2017

org, "Family members are defined as descendants, whether by birth or legal adoption, of Lambert and Annetje Van Valkenburg, who came to New Amsterdam from the Netherlands in 1643, and their spouses; and descendants of others of the surname Van Valkenburg, and their spouses. Variations in the spelling of Van Valkenburg shall not make anyone ineligible."[9]

There are also many organizations that have their own scholarships that some will find unusual, such as the Stuck at Prom Duct Tape Scholarship or the Florida Peanut Producers – you must own a peanut business to be eligible for the company's scholarship. If scholarships are too unique, then this means that most people are ineligible. Perhaps there is a left-handed club out there somewhere that may have a scholarship for any college, but for the most part, the odd ones are for very special circumstances only, and some are just myths.

---

9. The National Association of the Van Valkenburg Family, 2017

Apply, Apply, Apply!

s you begin your senior year in high school, it's time to gather information on scholarship applications. There are many reasons to choose a scholarship – and with the application process being different for each one, it's important not to get overwhelmed. Navigating the minefield of applications can be tricky, but hopefully this chapter settles your nerves and helps you apply for scholarships.

To prepare for college, seek advice from your school or future college academic advisor. These people are perfectly equipped to set you on the path to success! Advisors understand the importance of applying for scholarships early, how to apply for financial aid, and any other questions you may have. This chapter will help guide you through the process of applying in a quick and efficient way.

The Application Process

The previous chapter explored the types of scholarships that are available and where to find them. We will now concentrate on how to win those scholarships. There are specific things you can do to increase the likelihood of receiving a scholarship, including filling out your application correctly, writing a winning essay, and making sure your transcripts are in order. By making sure that you do it all the right way, you will increase your odds of winning a scholarship and bringing the money home, or to your dorm room!

Once you have decided on which colleges to apply to, the next step is to fill out the scholarship applications. Usually this is a straightforward process, but it can be time consuming. Most applications require similar information, so keep a folder for each school and make copies of everything — including admissions essays. This will prevent you from having to repeat your work for each school. Also, pay attention to admission deadlines. They can vary greatly from school to school, and you don't want to miss out on a scholarship just because you got the deadlines mixed up.

The admission packets are usually composed of most of these elements: the application, recommendations, essay, transcript, and interview.

Like pursuing any of your dreams, it takes time, effort, and planning to win a dream scholarship. Free money does not fall out of the sky — as much as we wish it did. You need to work for it and do the right things to increase the odds of getting it. So where do you start?

- Keep your information in a safe spot. Once you have thoroughly researched the many scholarships that you can apply for, gather all of the paperwork necessary to complete them. Keep it all in a safe spot.

- Know your deadlines. Make sure you know the deadlines and apply for each scholarship as early as you can. There is no sense in sending in your information if the deadline has come and gone. If you are unsure about whether the deadline is for mailing date or receipt date make sure that you send it early enough to be received by the listed date. When mailing, it can take up to seven days to get somewhere, even in the same town. If submitting electronically, do not wait until the last minute in case there is a problem with either your computer or the server. Early is always better than late, as late can disqualify you.

- Keep track of fees. There might be fees involved with photocopies, postage, and application fees, so make sure you keep track of money submitted by photocopying your check. Fees are unusual or normally minimal, but do your research before paying.

- Read the fine print. Before sending in your forms, read all the fine print to make sure that you have covered everything and followed ALL directions.

- Double-check everything. Check your application, essay, and any other paperwork for grammatical errors, content errors, and typos before you send it in. Do not rely on spell check! Double-check to make sure you have submitted everything and placed it in the correct order if specified. After writing the application, consider having a friend or family member review your writing. He or she can find accidental errors better than you because the content is fresh in their mind. If you're going the independent route, take a day to clear your mind before reading it aloud. You might catch something you missed!

- Do not leave spaces blank. Instead, write N/A or 0.

- Make sure you (or your counselor or parent) sign the form, if requested.

- Only include what is requested. Do not send in what was not required, like a résumé (most of what goes on an application is on your resume, so it is only repeating it) or extra letters of recommendations.

- Look for scholarships every year. There are usually new ones available.

Now that we have covered a few of the basics, we will go over what might be requested for your scholarship and how to make sure you have covered everything effectively.

Letters of Recommendation

Scholarship applications often require letters of recommendations. Even if they do not, it is a good idea to have a few in your pocket because you never know when you will need one. They come in handy in all kinds of situations, like college admission and job recommendations. You may need three to four letters of recommendation from different sources just for one scholarship application.

Recommendation letters are extremely important for winning a scholarship. Unfortunately, you must depend on someone else to help you with this part. Many students put it off until the last minute, and the person may not have time to write one or it won't be the best letter he or she could've written due to a lack of time. When you ask someone for a letter, always ask for it with plenty of notice. Two weeks is perfect, with a gentle reminder during the second week.

You should always choose the best person to write a reference letter. When you ask someone to write one for you, there are easy guidelines to remember. First, make sure you ask an adult who isn't related to you and who likes you. Never ask someone to write you a letter unless you know that they like and respect you. The best people to ask are the ones who have worked closely with you; they know you better than others and can usually write a more sincere letter.

Your recommendation letters also need to be well written. Some people just don't have the ability to give you a well-written letter, so it's always better to receive more letters than you need. This ensures that you can pick the best ones to send.

You should always give the writer a copy of your resume. While the writer may know you really well, they don't know everything about you. Your resume fills in the blanks for them and helps them write a better letter. It's also a good idea to sit down and talk with them if possible. Tell them more about yourself, and most importantly, let them know a few things about the scholarship application and what the committee is looking for.

EXAMPLE:
Student Request for Recommendation Letters

October 1, 2017

Dear Counselor or Teacher,

I would like to request your help with college admission Letters of Recommendation and Recommendation Forms. If you would, please complete forms and letters on my behalf for the colleges listed below. I really appreciate your help.

College	Requested Information
1. Two Rivers College	Recommendation Form – Online Common App.
2. Metropolitan University	"

3. Eureka University   "

4. Futures College   Paper Recommendation
                                             Form - attached

5. University of the Americas   Recommendation on
                                             school letterhead

For the online Common Application recommendation forms, I will "invite" you through the Common Application website in the next few days so you will be able submit the recommendations.

Regarding the paper recommendation forms, I would like to ask for these forms to be returned to me in "official" sealed envelopes so I can mail all my application materials together to each college (mailing the required documents in one envelope should reduce the chance of my paperwork getting lost). However, if you would rather mail the forms directly to each college, please let me know and I will be happy to provide self-addressed, stamped envelopes.

My college major will be Biology. My hope is to earn a degree that prepares me for a career in medicine. If you would, please include in your recommendations a discussion of my academic success, leadership role in science club, and the years of science and math tutoring I provided to elementary school students. These leadership and tutoring activities demonstrate a history of interest and involvement with people and science that I would like to communicate to college admissions officers.

In order to help you complete the requested forms and letters, I have included a copy of my student résumé. This résumé shows I am an all-around serious student and a contributing member of my school and community.

I would like to ask if you could submit my recommendations online or return the paper recommendations forms to me (or mail them directly to the colleges yourself) by October 27, 2017. Some of my college applications are due November 1, 2017 and I would like to make sure all supporting documents are completed by the required deadlines.

I will be available to answer questions anytime at school or at home (my e-mail is college4annaj@yahoo.com and my phone numbers are 555.555.1234 (home) and 555.555.4321 (cell)). Please let me know if there is anything I can do to help with this request.

Thank you, again.

Sincerely,

Anna Johnson

http://www.georgetownisd.org/cms/lib/TX01001838/Centricity/Domain/594/recommendation-letters-admission-cover.pdf

Next, you need to make copies of your letters, if possible. You still need to ask for a new letter for each scholarship so you can have an original signature and new date. An extra copy will help if the person is unavailable, and it can be reused, but only if it's also addressed in general (i.e.

"Dear Scholarship Committee…"), so you can send the copied letter if you're unable to get a new letter. If possible (unless the letter is given to you in a sealed envelope), proofread the letter yourself.

Generally, you'll need at least two letters from two teachers (or your school's staff), one from an administrator (this includes your principal, assistant principal, and/or your guidance counselor), and one from someone else. You can also ask an employer, your minister, or even a family doctor. If you can't get any of these, you can ask always your neighbors or even a family friend. Remember, family members can't write a letter of recommendation. While family might know you well, the scholarship committee won't accept their letter because it might be biased.

Always remember to sincerely thank the person who wrote the letter for you. When you've used the letter, it's a good idea to write them a short thank you note. Writing a good recommendation letter takes a lot of time, thought, and effort. Sometimes, it's the recommendation letter that sways the scholarship panel's decision.

The Essay

Of course, many scholarships ask for more than just letters of recommendation. Most ask that you write an essay (even if it is only 500 words or one to two paragraphs). Essays allow you to show off your grammatical and writing skills, as well as allow you to show off your unique voice and how well you can persuade or argue a point. Writing excellent scholarship essays is important to winning the scholarship, so we will cover this in detail.

Clarity, along with correct grammar, punctuation, and spelling are the essential foundations of an essay. Read the directions carefully before you begin writing. Never go over the word limit or under the minimum. Turning in an essay that is either too short or long can automatically disqualify you. Many applications ask for typed, double-spaced essays, and even stipulate a certain font or font size. If the directions aren't specific, remember that a typed, double-spaced essay with a simple font, like Times New Roman, is always best.

You need to make sure you clearly understand the essay topic or question. The opening sentence should grab the attention of the reader, making him or her want to read more. Above all, don't get off topic. You need to follow the main idea throughout the entire essay. Start out with an introduction that shows the panelist that you understand the essay's topic and back up your essay with examples or explanations.

Your personal experiences make the essay better. Whenever a student writes about overcoming obstacles — divorce, death, poverty, or even a type of disability — it displays strength and determination. Always finish with a strong conclusion that supports the main idea, something that can bring out a powerful emotion in the judges.

Always consider what the judges want. Find out what your audience's concerns are and write about it. If you cannot tie in that type of service, at least try to write about a similar kind of community service or experience. Don't go into religion or politics too deeply. There are so many different views on these controversial topics, and you don't want to insult someone's beliefs.

Fortunately for you, most scholarship essay questions are similar. The most popular question for seniors is, "What are your educational and career goals?" or some variation. You need to research the type of education needed for your chosen career, the number of years of education needed, and what you will financially need to get there. You also need to know what type of career opportunities your major will lead you to.

Write an essay that is approximately 500 words ahead of time, so you can either cut or add parts depending on the word count. When shortening the length, keep the most important parts and even use contractions when possible. When lengthening it, write more about your dreams and desires. If you still need more words, you can write in more detail about one of your examples in the essay, about an experience that led you to your career choice, or even an interview with someone who works in that field.

Because most scholarships are only awarded once, most committees don't check up on you at college to see if you majored in the field you wrote about, but you should still be truthful and write about your intended major. You can also write more passionately this way. Keep writing about the same major the entire year because many local scholarships have the same people on different scholarship committees.

Keep a copy of all your essays, so you can simply edit and re-edit most of them in a short amount of time. You should also keep any well-written essays that you wrote for a class assignment because some scholarships may have an unusual essay question that you'll be able to answer using an old essay as reference. You might even be able to use some of your college essays or parts of them for scholarship applications.

The Transcript

Transcripts are required for college applications but can also be requested by scholarship and grant committees. Transcripts are important, as they contain a record of all courses, grades, and degrees – especially for merit-based work – but you impress a scholarship committee with more than just your grades. Your essay, application, and letter of recommendation all factor in.

Transcripts are sent only at your request, so typically you have to sign a form that says you agree to release them and to where they will be released. A typical fee for transcripts is five dollars per copy of each official transcript that is sent out. Transcripts must be sent directly to the school or organization that is requesting them in order to be official. You can also request a copy for yourself, but that is considered "unofficial." It is a good idea to keep a copy of your transcripts on file for yourself, as you may need a copy to show at your scholarship interview. It is also a good idea to know what they look like.

You can generally request transcripts in several ways:

- By fax
- By mail or email
- In person

You can often request your transcripts online at your school. Normally there is a fee for transcripts, and many schools will not release them without pay. If you have several schools to get your transcripts from, it may behoove you to do it all at once. Refer to your list of application deadlines, and send the most time pressing ones first. Make a note of when you requested your transcripts. That way, if they do not arrive on time, you can call to find out if they were sent or got lost in the mail.

There are certain circumstances when transcripts will not be sent out, such as if a student has a hold on his or her records.

The Interview

Some scholarships, just like college entrance requirements, request an interview. We will now examine the interview process and go over what is expected of you and how to make it smoother. Keep the information in mind for other interviews you may have — from job interviews to college entrance interviews — as the process is usually similar for each of these.

Some, but not all, scholarships require an interview. Often, the more competitive the scholarship is or the more prestigious the school awarding the scholarship is, the more rigorous the process is for getting the money. That may include an interview in person or by phone or even webcam if you do not live near them. There are several ways in which to conduct an interview, and they can all vary in procedure. Some are more casual in nature with just one or two people in the room, while others could be more formal and extensive with a panel of members waiting their turn to ask you questions. A scholarship interview can be intimidating, but the better prepared you are, the less intimidating it will be.

How to prepare before the interview:

- Bring a copy of the paperwork: It is best to bring along a copy of all of your scholarship paperwork that was submitted to the scholarship committee, such as your essay, transcripts, and application.

- Review materials: Review your scholarship materials before you have an interview. You may be applying for many scholarships, and you want to be sure that you are familiar with the one that you are dealing with now.

- Re-read the original scholarship application request: Think about what the scholarship committee might be looking for in a candidate, and be prepared. Research the organization that is awarding the scholarship so that you know what they stand for and believe in.

- Make notes: Make notes to yourself about any details that could help you refresh your thoughts. Keep a copy on hand to review the day before the interview.

- Practice for your interview: Practice with family or friends. You could even videotape yourself to see how you spoke and how your body language was during a practice interview.

- Know the location: Make sure you know where the interview is. Get your directions ahead of time. Never be late. It is always best to be a few minutes early. Leave early in case of heavy traffic or other unforeseen circumstances.

- Know where to park: If the interview paperwork does not state where to park, perhaps you can contact someone at the organization to ask where to park and if there are any parking fees. Bring money just in case you must park somewhere with meters or other fees.

- Bring contact information with you: In case of an emergency, such as car trouble, you want to be able to call if there is a delay.

- Get a good night's rest the night before: It will keep you alert and refreshed.

- Eat beforehand: You do not want to think about hunger pangs during your interview or have your stomach growling. Make sure you eat a good meal before you go and bring along a snack, such as a granola bar, just in case you need an energy boost.

- Wear something professional: You do not need to go overboard, but dress nice. No jeans, T-shirts, or flip flops. You must dress business casual! For men, this generally means no suit or jeans. Consider wearing dress pants, a button-down shirt, and casual dress shoes. For women, avoids jeans, but don't opt for a prom dress! Women have more options for business casual, including dresses – not cotton – dress pants, jackets, cardigans, sweaters, heels or flats.

- Arrive early: Ten to 15 minutes early is a good amount of time.

- Turn off your cellphone (or leave it in your car): Even when it is on vibrate it can still be heard.

During the interview:

- Do not forget to breathe deeply: It will relax you so you can concentrate on your thoughts.

- Always greet each interviewer with a firm handshake and hello.

- Make eye contact with your interviewers: When someone is speaking to you, look back at him or her.

- It never hurts to smile: Smiling shows off your personality.

- Sit up straight, and watch your body language: Do not slump or fidget.

- Listen carefully to the questions before you answer each.

- You do not have to rush your answers: You can take your time to formulate your thoughts.

- Do not give just a "yes" or "no" answer: Explain yourself. At the same time, do not go on and on either.

- Be honest: Lying is not going to get you anywhere except the rejection list.

- Show pride in your accomplishments: Do not be pompous and arrogant, but do not hide what you should show off.

- Ask for clarification if you do not understand something: It is okay to have the committee rephrase or restate something for you.

- If you do not know the answer to a question, you are better off telling them that you honestly do not know, rather than making something up.

- Do not be afraid to ask questions about the process, the scholarship, or anything else.

- Thank the interviewers for their time: They will appreciate it. If you can, send a note of thanks afterwards.

What might the interviewers ask?

- You may be asked about your background: Where you were born and raised? What was your first job?

- You may be asked about your school records, your ranking, and what your GPA is.

- You may be asked about what classes you took previously and how they apply to your field of study.

- You may be asked if you have hobbies, pastimes, or do any volunteer work.

- You may be asked about your five-year goals, your 10-year goals, and your lifetime goals.

- You may be asked about your financial picture and how you plan to pay for schooling, or if you plan on working at all.

- You may be asked about your family and who they are.

- You may be asked about where you plan to reside after college and what job you will be aiming for.

- You may be asked to role-play and answer questions as to what your reaction would be to "such and such," or what you would do in a particular situation.

- You may be asked to describe how your peers see you, or how you see yourself; such as describe yourself in one or two words.

- You may be asked about a person or event that impacted you.

- As you can see, there are few limits to what you might be asked, but generally the interviewers are trying to get a sense of who you are and where you are headed, and how the scholarship will help you get there.

Wrapping It Up

Finding a scholarship is only half the battle. Once you find it, you may still have a long road ahead of you to get scholarship funds. You might have to fill out a lengthy application, write a several-page essay, or make it through an interview with a scholarship committee. You will have to apply and apply, and you will not win everyone that you apply for, but do not give up. While it all seems daunting, stressful, and time-consuming, if you break down your scholarship requirements into steps and concentrate on one thing at a time, it is not so bad. Getting free money takes time and effort, but in the end, you will be glad you went through the process, especially when you are finished with college and possibly looking at a stack of student loans to pay.

Chapter 5

FAFSA And Grants

The Free Application for Federal Student Aid (FAFSA) is one of the most important applications you will encounter. Schools, government agencies, many financial aid officers, and others determine your need based off your Student Aid Report (SAR) since this is the best way to ensure that you get all that you deserve.

Private colleges may use a different financial aid application called the College Board's CSS/Financial Aid PROFILE application. Some colleges require additional forms that must be filled out and sent directly to that school. In short, you should find out for each school that you are applying to exactly what their requirements are for financial aid applications.

Alongside FAFSA, grants are a great way to cut the costs of college since this money does not have to be returned. While scholarships are generally based on performance, grants are often based on need. Grants can range from $100 to full tuition costs at a four-year college or university. Consider going the FAFSA and grant route since paying back loan money can take years, and even put you behind in your dream career. It is in your best interest to take advantage of all the free money which you can receive. Most students end up wishing they had borrowed less, as the payments can be very hard to manage.

What Is FAFSA?

The Free Application for Federal Student Aid (FAFSA) is a federally funded, nationwide program, even though each state has its own type of state grants, scholarships, and loans. The FAFSA has its own rules for grants and loans, which are based on financial need. I've learned some useful information about this program that may benefit you, no matter what state you live in.

FAFSA is a financial-need application that must be renewed annually, no matter what your income is. It's based on your parents' income and yours (if you filed taxes) from the previous year. Besides the amount of your adjusted gross income FAFSA takes into consideration the number of people living in your household and immediate family members (also in your household) attending college. They don't take into consideration the normal bills (rent/mortgage, utilities, phone, gas, etc.) everyone must pay.

The FAFSA is a form that documents important facts about you and your family's financial situation, including income and assets. Essentially, colleges have an allotted amount of money for their students, and they use FAFSA to ration aid to the families who need it most.

You are not going to know the exact amount of financial aid you will receive until April. There you can get an estimate of your potential grant money. Your financial need is the Cost of Attendance (COA), minus your Expected Family Contribution (EFC), which is the amount that you and your family are expected to pay out of pocket for your receive. The goal here is to follow strategies to reduce your EFC to the minimum, which will increase the amount of aid you will be eligible to receive. Here is the good news: your EFC doesn't increase if the COA increases, so if you choose a more expensive school, you are actually eligible for more aid.

EXAMPLE OF FINANCIAL NEED DETERMINATION:

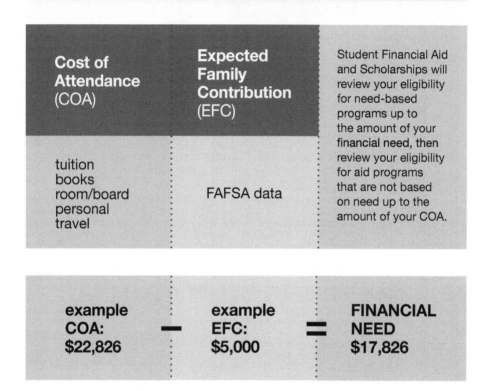

Cost of Attendance (COA)	Expected Family Contribution (EFC)	Student Financial Aid and Scholarships will review your eligibility for need-based programs up to the amount of your financial need, then review your eligibility for aid programs that are not based on need up to the amount of your COA.
tuition books room/board personal travel	FAFSA data	

example COA: $22,826	**—**	example EFC: $5,000	**=**	FINANCIAL NEED $17,826

Worksheets are available online at **www.finaid.org/calculators**. These can help you get organized and learn how the process works.

The Student Aid Report (SAR) from the FAFSA is sent to you, as well your college choices, and then the financial aid office determines the amount you'll receive, and whether it will be a grant (which you don't pay back) or a low-interest rate loan. There are two different types of student loans: subsidized loans, in which interest starts after graduation, or unsubsidized loans, where the interest is paid while you are in college.

If your loan need is greater than what they will lend a student, there are also parent plus loans, where the parent pays a monthly fee upon receiving the loan. All of these loans do have certain requirements, such as the amount and your credit. But as this is a book on scholarships and ways to avoid loans, you can go to either your college's financial aid department or online to **www.FAFSA.ed.gov** for more information on loan conditions.

If you've had a change that's affected the upcoming school year versus the previous year, the financial aid office will usually work with you and readjust your amount of grants or loans you receive. For example, you'll be attending college in fall 2018, and the application is filled out with 2017 tax forms. If your income for 2018 drops by a good amount, perhaps because of job loss, divorce, a death in the family, a huge hospital bill, or new financial care for an elderly relative, then you should contact the college's financial aid office and let them know. They may ask for something in writing, such as a notarized paper, or even a paycheck stub, but they'll generally help you out. It never hurts to ask.

A student must use his or her parents' income for the FAFSA if he or she depends on them. There are a few cases where a student is independent, however, it's difficult to verify this. If a parent refuses to help pay for his or her child's college expenses or tells him or her to move out, the student still has to list their parent's income until age 25. If the student gets married or is in the armed forces before 25, then they will be declared independent. Students can also be independent if they are pregnant or have a child, but they must prove that they pay for over 50 percent of the baby's expenses. Students can also become emancipated, but it takes time, work, and must be accepted by the courts as well.

There are some other circumstances where students can declare themselves as independent. For example, if the student is a ward of the court or foster child, they're considered independent. With the amount of homeless people growing over the past few years, students can declare themselves "homeless" (their family may live with another family, in a hotel, or at a homeless shelter) and are considered independent from then on. If the high school is aware of situations like this, then declaring independence is much easier if you can get the school to make it official on the student's transcripts.

How to Apply for FAFSA

You need to fill out the Federal Application for Free Student Aid form as soon as possible, especially if you're eligible for financial need. You cannot apply until January of the year you will be attending college in the fall. Once again, you need to reapply every year. Each school gets so much money from the government, and you need to try and get it before they hand it all out. One financial aid officer told me that the first applications receive larger amounts of money than the late ones. If you're attending college in the summer before July 1 of any year, then you need to fill out a FAFSA form from the previous year – for example, the 2018-2019 application using your 2017 income.

Financial aid offices should have the FAFSA application for you. but if you apply online you'll receive your results much faster. Staff members can also help you fill out paperwork if needed. You need to be careful when you apply online, and make sure you're on the correct website. When you google FAFSA, the first website is FAFSA.com (which is not the official government website.) Don't pay anything—FAFSA is FREE, and the first two letters, FA, in FAFSA stand for "free application". Just make sure that you go to **www.FAFSA.ed.gov**.

The FAFSA form is available from many sources, but the best way to do it is online. Your results will be sent to you and the colleges much faster if you complete the online form, and the IRS Data Retrieval Tool, which FAFSA uses to work with your income, also makes the procedure much easier. Another reason to use the Retrieval Tool is that approximately 30 percent of all FAFSAs are selected for verification (meaning the student/parent must provide paper proof of everything), and the ones that do not use the IRS Data Retrieval Tool are usually the first ones chosen.

Filing your FAFSA online will get you your SAR a few weeks earlier than if you used the paper version. The Web version also has a built-in error-check system and makes it easier to file a Renewal FAFSA, which you must do every year.

In the past, the Web version required that you get a Personal Identification Number (PIN). Beginning in 2016, applicants no longer use PIN numbers. Instead, you will create a Federal Student Aid ID with a username and password. Parents will be able to use the same username and password for their children.

When you are ready to start, you need to get your financial documents together. You are going to need, at a minimum:

- Your driver's license and Social Security card

- Your income tax returns for the previous year.
  If you are married, you will also need your spouse's returns.
- Your parents' income tax returns for the previous year
- Your parents' Social Security numbers
- Recent bank statements
- Statements relating to stocks, bonds, mutual funds, tuition plans, Section 529 savings plans, and Coverdell Education Savings Accounts
- Statements showing nontaxable income such as Veteran's Benefits, Social Security income, or AFDC
- Family-owned business and farm records

Filling out the FAFSA is a lot like doing your taxes. If your family has always paid someone to prepare your taxes and never really paid attention to the result, you might have some trouble with the terminology. Follow the instructions, and you should be fine. Unless you have complicated business finances, you should be able to complete the form in a couple of hours.

When you are filling out the forms, be careful to avoid these common mistakes:

- Do not leave any blanks. If the question does not apply to your situation, enter "0".

- Include in your untaxed income, any Earned Income Credit you received, or retirement fund contributions you made.

- Be sure to answer questions about your parents' education. If you are a first-generation college student, you might qualify for a state grant.

- Always answer "yes" when asked about the different kinds of aid you are interested in, even if you are not. Answering "no" is not going to get more grant money.

- You will be asked a question about which federal income tax form you filed — 1040, 1040A, or 1040EZ. What this question is actually asking is which form you are eligible to file, which can make a difference in the amount of aid you will receive. Enter 1040A or 1040EZ, unless you had no choice but file the 1040.

- Do not skip worksheets A, B, and C, which appear at the end of the application.

Double-check everything, and, as always, print or keep a copy. The first one is the hard one. The Renewal FAFSA, which you will complete in subsequent years, mostly involves putting in any changes to your income and expenses.

What Are Grants?

Since grants are one of the most efficient ways to cover the cost of tuition, let's have a look at what grants are, and how you can receive their benefits. A good place to start looking for grant information is with the financial aid office of the college you will be attending. You should contact your state's Department of Education to find out if there are any grants you may be eligible for. There are also websites that can help you track down grants that may be available from private sources, which we will explore shortly. Private sources may be companies that are using grants for college as public relations tools (while utilizing the possible tax deduction), or they may be offered by a private individual that is trying to assist certain kinds of students with certain kinds of needs.

For instance, the grant may be designed for American Indian students who are planning to use their studies to help on a reservation. They may be specific, such as a grant designed for single mothers studying dentistry, or they may be broad, such as art students who are working on their BFA degree at a specific art college.

If you look hard enough, you will certainly find a grant for which you are qualified to apply. One is a popular site that many college financial aid offices recommend as a supplemental source to find and apply for private grants is **www.fastweb.com**.

Although many of the available grants are given out according to financial need, some grants are merit-based, while others are designed to promote a particular field of study or to encourage students to attend private schools. They may be even be based on ethnicity, religion, or association. You might discover grants that require a high GPA for a particular field of study, such as math or science. There are plenty of private grants out there, and you may be qualified for more than one. Private grants can be used in addition to government grants, both of which we will go over in more detail shortly.

Grants, whether private- or government-funded, are created to help you reduce the costs of college. They are not designed to be used for a vacation to Bermuda, a new stereo system for your dorm room, a down payment on a new vehicle, or new clothing for your wardrobe. They are specifically intended to be used for paying the funds to the school directly, so the money never reaches your hands. You might have to pay a portion of that financial aid back (especially if the aid is through the federal government), depending on the date.

As with all your financial planning for college, be sure to apply for grants early because funds are limited. Every deadline differs, but it is generally a good idea to get all of your financial applications in by Feb. 15.

TYPES OF GRANTS

- Federal Pell grants
- Federal Supplemental Educational Opportunity Grants (FSEOGs)
- Teacher Education Assistance for College and Higher Education (TEACH)
- Iraq and Afghanistan service grants
- Grants for American Indians, Alaska natives, and native Hawaiians
- State-based college grants

Different types of grants include:

Federal Grants

Federal grants are, by definition, an award of financial assistance from a federal agency. To see if you qualify for this grant, you will want to fill out the FAFSA form. Remember, you can find the form at high schools and college financial aid offices; you can fill the form out online at **www. fafsa.ed.gov,** or by calling the Federal Student Aid, an office of the U.S. Department of Education, at 1-800-4-FED-AID (1-800-433-3243).

Again, make sure you file the form as early as possible, as some grants have limited funds for the year.

Pell Grants

Pell Grants provide more than 90 percent of all federal grant money (veterans' benefits excluded). They are awarded to undergraduates who have not received a bachelor's degree. Pell Grants are based on the financial needs of the applicant, taking into consideration the size of the student's household, the amount of their yearly income, and depending on the college, the cost of tuition at the school the student has chosen.

This information is based on what you submit on the FAFSA. The maximum amount of a Pell Grant per award year is $4,050, although the maximum amount every year is based on funding. You may receive the Pell Grant for every year that you work toward your bachelor's degree, as there is no limit on the number of times you receive it as long as you qualify. However, you may only receive one Pell Grant per year, although the funds received are paid by semesters.

Some of the eligibility requirements to receive a Pell Grant include:

- You must demonstrate a financial need by submitting FAFSA.
- You must be a U.S. citizen or an eligible noncitizen.
- You must have a high school diploma or a GED.
- You must not have defaulted on any student loans.
- You must have a valid Social Security Number.
- You must be enrolled in an eligible postsecondary school.
- You must be working toward a first undergraduate degree or teaching credential.

- Male applicants must have registered for the Selective Service, if they are between the ages of 18 and 25.
- Satisfactory academic progress must be maintained.
- You must certify that the funds will be used only for educational purposes.

Academic Competitiveness Grant and National SMART Grants

According to the U.S. Department of Education, two grants are available to those that are studying topics in math, science, technology, engineering, and critical foreign languages: The Academic Competitiveness Grant (ACG) and National Science and Mathematics Access to Retain Talent (National SMART Grant) Programs. These are performance-based and are awarded to those who have demonstrated a financial need.

If you are in your first or second academic year of college, you may be eligible for the Academic Competitiveness Grant and receive up to $750 for the first year of study and up to $1,300 for the second year. During your third and fourth academic years, you may be eligible for a National SMART Grant and receive up to $4,000 for each year of study.

Requirements for Academic Competitiveness Grant and National SMART Grants are, for each year of study:

- You must be a U.S. citizen.
- You must be attending school full-time in a four-year degree-granting institution.
- You must be eligible to receive a Pell Grant.
- You must meet other eligibility requirements related to — depending on your year in school — completing a rigorous high school curriculum; majoring in mathematics, science, or selected foreign languages; and maintaining a required GPA.

Supplemental Educational Opportunity Grants

Other federal grants that are need-based are the Federal Supplemental Education Opportunity Grants (FSEOG). FSEO grants range from $100 to $4,000 and are distributed at least once per term.

The grants are designed for undergraduates or vocational students who are enrolled in school at least half-time, and are pursuing their first bachelor's degree and have exceptional financial need. Students who are already receiving a Pell Grant are given priority to receive a FSEOG. Determination is made by Expected Family Contribution (EFC) score, which was determined on their financial aid application. Check with your school's financial aid office for more details about the FSEOG.

Leveraging Educational Assistance Partnership (LEAP)

The Leveraging Educational Assistance Partnership is also known as the "LEAP Program." Instead of providing grants directly to students, the program provides grants to states to help them provide their own-need based grants. Both undergraduate and graduate students, who must demonstrate a large financial need, may apply for the program in the state they reside in. Some of the eligibility requirements for the program are:

- You must demonstrate financial need.
- You must be eligible to receive the Pell Grant.
- You must be a U.S. citizen or an eligible noncitizen.
- You must not have defaulted on any student loans.
- Male applicants must have registered for the Selective Service.
- Satisfactory academic progress must be maintained.

In addition to the LEAP Program, there is the SLEAP Program, which is available to states that participate in the LEAP Program. According to the U.S. Department of Education, "The SLEAP Program assists states in providing education and who have substantial financial need. The student aid programs can be in the form of supplemental grants, supplemental community service work-study employment, or merit and academic achievement or critical career scholarships." Both undergraduate and graduate students with financial need student aid programs can be in the form of supplemental grants, supplemental community service work-study employment, or merit and academic achievement or critical career scholarships." Both undergraduate and graduate students with financial needs may apply to their residential state.

For more information, visit **www.ed.gov**, call the Federal Student Aid Information Center at 800-433-3243 or 800- 4FED-AID, or ask your school's financial aid office.

Federal Agency Grants

Federal agency grants are grants that come from places like the National Endowment for the Arts, an independent federal agency. Federal agency grants are awarded for reasons other than education. These grants are designed for everyone, from small businesses, to organizations, to individuals, all of which you can easily research **www.grants.gov**. According to Grants.gov, the federal agencies that provide grants include:

- Agency for International Development
- Corporation for National and Community Service
- Department of Agriculture
- Department of Commerce
- Department of Defense
- Department of Education
- Department of Energy
- Department of Health and Human Services
- Department of Homeland Security
- Department of Housing and Urban Development
- Department of the Interior
- Department of Justice
- Department of Labor
- Department of State
- Department of Transportation
- Department of the Treasury
- Department of Veterans Affairs
- Environmental Protection Agency

- Institute of Museum and Library Services
- National Aeronautics and Space
- National Archives and Records Administration
- National Endowment for the Arts
- National Endowment for the Humanities
- National Science Foundation
- Small Business Administration
- Social Security Administration

State Grants

Most states have grant programs to help with college, however, like many grants they are often need-based. Keep in mind that some states have signed reciprocity agreements with other states to offer need-based grant programs to out-of-state undergraduates; it is something to consider if you are a resident in a state other than where you are attending college.

For example, in Florida, residents can apply for the Florida Bright Futures Scholarship Program, a program that establishes three lottery-funded scholarships to reward high school graduates for academic achievement. They can apply for other funds, such as the José Martí Scholarship Challenge Grant Fund and receive $2,000 per year. This need-based merit award is designed for eligible students of Hispanic origin who will attend Florida public or eligible private institutions and are enrolled in a minimum of 12 credit hours for undergraduate study or 9 credit hours for graduate study. For more information, contact the Florida Department of Education's Office of Student Financial Assistance at 888-827-2004 or visit **www.floridastudentfinancialaid.org**, or check with your school's financial aid office.

Wrapping It Up

Keep in mind that because these programs come from the government, the rules can change. For example, in recent years rule changes have made it harder to become eligible for the Pell Grant.

Grants are a great way to help pay for your college education, and you will not have to worry about paying it back. Your student loan payments will not be so hefty, and you will have fewer financial worries while in school.

Do not assume that you are not qualified for a grant; always check with your school's financial aid office to see if you might be eligible. Generally, they will have much of the necessary paperwork to apply for government grants. For private grants, you might check out **www. fastweb.com**.

There are need-based and merit-based grants especially designed for women, minorities, undergraduates, graduates, doctoral students, and more. With a little research, you can no doubt find grants and other "free money" that you are eligible to receive.

Chapter 6

Saving Money & Living Cheap

There are a few other ways to fund your college education besides scholarships and loans. Once you've decided on your future college, consider where you'll live, how you'll get to class, and the overall cost of tuition.

Visit Campuses

Before you settle on one school, visit the campus for a couple of days. Since you are going to spend two to four years (or possibly more) and make a considerable financial investment, it is a good idea to make sure it is right for you. Visiting the actual college can completely change your mind, as each college has a personality of its own.

Before you arrive, prepare a list of questions that can help you decide if the school is right for you. Your list might include:

- How much can you expect to pay for rent and utilities for off-campus housing?
- What types of scholarships or grants are offered?
- Are part-time jobs available near campus?
- What is the availability and cost of public transportation?
- Do other students look like those you want to spend your next few years with? Does it seem to be a close-knit community? What is the cultural diversity of the student body?
- Can you imagine yourself on campus? Does it feel right?
- Is there campus security available, especially for night classes? You might ask about the crime rate.

- What is on the bulletin boards and in the college papers? What kinds of topics are the students discussing?
- What does the campus look like? Is it clean or dirty? New or rundown?
- How large are the classes?
- What services does the school offer? Job placement? Academic advising? Internships?
- What is the quality of the teachers? What is the average number of students per class?
- What are some of the extracurricular activities?

Cost

Should you receive financial aid to attend college, it is possible that a private school will turn out to cost the same as a state school. Apply to all schools that you like, and apply to every possible source of financial help. As a precaution, choose a fallback school, one where you are guaranteed admittance. It should also be affordable so that you can attend and get your degree if you get only a small amount of loans.

Calculating the Real Cost

Once you have narrowed your choices down and have some idea of where you are headed, it is time to face the reality of finances.

- **Tuition:** A big up-front cost is, of course, tuition. This is the money the college charges you to attend classes, and it is usually based on a semester. Remember that tuition tends to increase about eight percent per year, so if you are planning a couple of years in advance, adjust this cost accordingly.

- **Fees:** This can be a tricky one. Colleges charge a variety of fees for all kinds of services. First, there are the fees that are built into the tuition per credit hour. These fees include things such as transportation access, technology, sports, and activities. Parking at urban colleges can cost as much as $500 per year for the privilege of driving your car. You will also have to pay a health fee, which covers doctor's visits at the school's clinic. Be sure to read over carefully what the health fee does and does not cover. For example, you usually have to pay full price for prescriptions unless you have insurance.

- **Books:** College textbooks are notoriously expensive. Costs vary by course, but you can expect to pay $300-$500 per semester. You are also going to need notebooks, pencils and pens, a calculator, and the usual school supplies. More information about purchasing cheap books will be discussed later in this chapter.

- **Living expenses (on-campus):** If you choose to live in a dormitory, living expenses are easy to figure. Just be sure to check if the meal plan includes weekends and calculate accordingly. Also, if you plan to stay in the dorms in the summer, there will be an additional charge.

- **Living expenses (off-campus):** You should include the cost of rent, utilities, phone and internet, and groceries. You should also include any deposits you will have to pay, which can be considerable for first-time renters. If you have a roommate, these expenses can be cut in half.

- **Computer:** These days, a computer is a necessity. For the greatest flexibility, you should choose a laptop. You can take it with you to classes, to the library, home with you on the weekends or on breaks, or wherever you need. Most schools offer free computer labs that you can use, but the inconvenience generally is not worth it. When choosing a computer, you should get one with enough memory and speed to get you through four years of college. Do not skimp on performance just to save a few dollars because it may cost you in the long run. You should also consider the cost of software as well, which is going to vary according to which major you choose to study.

- **Clothes and entertainment:** This is where a lot of your disposable income is going to go, but it can be difficult to budget. Ask your parents what they spend on your clothing per year to get some idea of how much you can expect to spend. College towns have many opportunities for you to eat, drink, and be merry, but also many opportunities to leave you broke. Be sure to include some money for the occasional splurge.

- **Insurance:** Generally, your parents' health insurance will continue to cover you while you are in school, and if they have a family plan there is no additional cost to keep you signed up. If you are not covered, you should consider getting your own health insurance. Costs vary, and many colleges offer an affordable plan designed specifically for students.

- **Cell phone, cable TV:** You are probably going to be willing to pay for the convenience of a cell phone. It is a luxury, not a necessity, but everyone has become so used to carrying one around that they think they are a necessity. The same goes for cable TV. Chances are, your dorm room is going to have a common area with a TV – so consider not getting your own TV to cut costs.

- **Household items:** Whether you are living in the dorms or an apartment off campus, you are going to have to consider the essentials of daily life. You can probably bring some of this from home, provided your parents will let you, but be sure to estimate the cost of what you may have to purchase.

  - Blankets, sheets, towels, and washcloths
  - Soap, deodorant, shampoo, toothpaste, and other grooming products
  - Appliances, such as a coffee maker, small microwave oven, and toaster (or toaster oven)
  - Food — if you do not live in the dorms, or your meal plan does not cover all of your meals

Budget Worksheet for College Students

INCOME:	Daily	Monthly	Semesterly	Yearly
From Jobs (after taxes)				
From Parents / Family				
From Financial Aid				
Miscellaneous Income				
Other				
Total Income:				

FIXED EXPENSES:	Daily	Monthly	Semesterly	Yearly
Rent / Housing				
Food / Meal Plan				
Car Payment				
Car Insurance & Registration				
Tuition & Fees				
Loan / Credit Card Payments				
Telephone / Cell Phone				
Utilities				
Other				
Total Fixed Expenses:				

FLEXIBLE EXPENSES:	Daily	Monthly	Semesterly	Yearly
Eating Out				
Clothing				
Books				
Entertainment				
Public Transportation				
Cable				
Internet Access				
Personal Hygiene Items (Shampoo, deodorant, etc.)				
Recreation				
Miscellaneous				
Gym				
Child Care				
Laundry / Dry Cleaning				
Travel				
Savings				
Other				
Total Flexible Expenses:				

	Daily	Monthly	Semesterly	Yearly
Total Income:				
Total Fixed Expenses:				
Total Flexible Expenses:				
Balance:				

https://www.tidyform.com/download/budget-worksheet-for-college-students/
redirect/xlsx.html

Add these figures, and try to think of anything else you might need, or anything else you will be doing that will require extra money.

These expenses can add up to a scary total that goes way beyond financial aid goals.

It is important to do this exercise for each school to which you are going to apply. Costs vary widely, and you cannot assume that the price of a dorm room at one school is going to be same as the price at another. Many schools even charge different prices based on which dorm you end up living in. The more expensive ones usually have more amenities, such as a larger or private bedroom, less people to the bathrooms, and even a gym. But again, do you need all of this? Is it worth the extra costs?

There are also many professions that require you to have a degree. Even if you end up doing something else with your life than what you studied in college, your degree is going to open doors for you your whole life that would otherwise remain closed.

Public versus Private

One of the options you will have to consider when choosing a school is whether to attend a private school or a state-funded college. There are advantages and disadvantages to each.

A diploma from a private school traditionally carries more prestige than one from a public school, but this is mainly the Ivy League schools, such as Harvard, Princeton, and Brown. Recruiters and graduate school committees have customarily looked favorably upon such private schools. However, as with any degree, there are no guarantees. A fancy pedigree may not help you succeed.

As always, before you decide on a school because of its name recognition, do your homework, and make sure the reality matches the hype. You might find some surprises.

Private schools can offer options or alternative curricula that are not available at public schools. Small private schools are often founded with guiding principles or beliefs that set them apart. Smaller schools have also made themselves more attractive (and therefore competitive) by offering small class sizes, unusual course requirements, or interesting social programs. If you are the kind of person who likes to wander off the beaten track, then a private school might get you there.

The reason many students do not consider applying to private schools is that they are more expensive than public schools. Private schools' costs may be more reasonable than you think. At the same time, many of these private schools will offer huge scholarships that only make a small dent in the costs. When the total cost comes into play, oftentimes their tuition is so high that you will still end up paying much more to go there than a public school.

Many of the Ivy League schools are more easily affordable if you are in financial need. Princeton was one of the first to do this, and more now follow this path. Of course, you still have to meet the requirements to be accepted, but quite a few private schools do not want their students to have loans and will give them scholarships and grants to help cover the costs. They will still look at what the FAFSA considers to be the parents' contribution, so this all relies on having a low income.

In-State versus Out-of-State

What if you choose the public-school route, but the school you want to attend is in a different state? An out-of-state public school might also offer a certain program of study that is not available in your state.

Be prepared to pay. Public schools are funded in part by tax dollars, so if you live in a different state you will be expected to pay this portion as additional tuition. Out-of-state tuition can actually be three times the amount of in-state tuition, and most states have toughened up their policies in recent years.

If it truly is your dream to attend an out-of-state school, ask the school's financial aid office about residency requirements. Some schools allow you to establish residency after you have attended for a certain period, but generally this involves living off-campus. You probably will also be required to file a tax return in that state, and register your car there. Before this happens, be prepared to work extra hard to come up with additional funds.

Location Matters

The type of environment that the school is located in can have a great effect on the cost of your education. Rent tends to be high for schools located in urban areas.

Location also has a big effect on your transportation costs. If you plan to drive home often, the farther away you are the more it is going to cost. If the school is too far away to drive, you will probably want to fly home several times a year, which can be costly.

If you do not have or want to have to buy a car, you may want to consider what kind of public transportation is available. Check with the city's public transportation department to see if buses are readily available and how often they run. You might want to see how often they come and go near your school. A few cities, such as New York, San Francisco, and Chicago offer the bonus of being able to take trains and cabs, if you can afford them.

An additional consideration for location is climate. If you are accustomed to the sunny warmth of Florida, a Wisconsin winter is going to be a real shock. If you prefer a mild climate, then you are not going to enjoy the heat and humidity of South Carolina. It seems like a small consideration, but remember, you are going to have to live there for four years. Plus, if you do not have the clothing, that is another consideration. If you live in a warm climate and do not have warm sweaters, jackets, boots, and mittens, that can add up to hundreds of dollars that you have to dole out just to go to college.

CASE STUDY: Kristen Joseph

When I began my college search, the two main things that I judged every option against were affordability and ambiance. My parents are far from wealthy, and while they took amazing care of my siblings, and me they were never able to save up any extra money for college expenses. I had a job and continually applied to different scholarships, but the prospect of not being able to afford college was still worrisome. So naturally, I wanted to go to a school that would offer me enough financial aid to cover almost all of my expenses. And, with any luck, that school would have a campus culture that I felt comfortable in (and buildings that looked similar to the Hogwarts castle in Harry Potter, because I have a penchant for gothic architecture).

Fast-forward to college acceptance letter season. I had applied to six schools, and had gotten into most of them, but I was still waiting on the status of my application at my dream school, the University of Chicago. With a gorgeous campus, delightfully quirky culture, top tier academics, and proximity to a major city, this school had it all. The only problem: I didn't think they would accept me. Sure, I was in the top ten percent of my graduating class academically, but UChicago only accepts the top seven percent of applicants in the entire nation! Not to mention the fact that the price tag on this school was the most expensive that I had seen anywhere, with a cost of attendance that is the same for both in-state and out-of-state students.

I had already resigned myself to the belief that I wouldn't be going there — even if I did receive an acceptance letter from UChicago, there was no way I would be able to afford the cost of attendance . . . so you can imagine my surprise when I not only received an acceptance letter from the University of Chicago, but also a financial aid package that covered the complete cost of attendance without making me take out any loans!

I was shocked, but also very excited. I would be able to afford my dream school! I still took out a very small loan to cover out-of-pocket costs like non-dining-hall food and flights back home during breaks. My family and I did the 16-hour drive from Florida to Chicago, Illinois, for my orientation weekend. I'm glad we got there safely, but I never want to drive that route again; we encountered everything from flat tires to highways riddled with potholes on the way up, so you can trust me when I say that flying is a much better option if you live more than a couple hours' drive from your school. It's also very important to make sure that you have weather-appropriate clothing. For example, the Midwest winters are actually bearable for this Florida girl because of puffy coats, winter boots, warm hats, and thick leggings under my jeans.

All in all, I'm very happy with where I ended up. The campus is beautiful, the academics are adequately challenging, and I've made some great friends and definitely feel like I belong there. I never thought I'd be able to go to the University of Chicago, yet here I am today. I guess that just goes to show that attending your dream school is actually an attainable goal.

Kristen Joseph, Editorial Intern at Atlantic Publishing Group, is a second-year student at the University of Chicago.

Living at Home

One of the best ways to cut the cost of attending college is to live at home. This option is not for everyone, of course. Some students do not live within commuting distance of a desirable college. Most students, though, simply do not want to live at home. Being on your own is part of the college experience and is one that many students loathe giving up. There definitely are advantages to living on-campus or near school: friendships are easier to make and sustain, and you will feel more a part of the college community.

The main advantage to living at home is that your parents are probably footing the bills. Many times, living can cost much more than tuition. If you do decide to face the situation and go it on the cheap, there are some hazards to watch out for. Although it may be cheap, living at home and going to school may not necessarily be easy.

If your parents are pressed for cash, you may want to consider making an arrangement with them that you pay rent for living at their house. The rent, no doubt, would still be less than if you were out on your own somewhere else.

Commuter Blues

Driving to school can be a real burden. Parking is the first problem. Most schools grow faster than their parking lots, which means when school begins in the fall you might find yourself driving onto curbs or parking your car in the street to make it to class because there are no spaces available. The situation tends to ease in the afternoon and evening, when fewer students are in class. This schedule could take some getting used to, but it will relieve many headaches for you. An additional option is to take the earliest classes, which are not very popular. This will get you into a parking space before the rush begins at 9 a.m.

Keep in mind that commuting to school is not free. First, with the price of gas fluctuating, the daily drive to college or home can add up. Calculate how much fuel is going to cost. Also, keep in mind that commuting is going to add wear and tear to your vehicle. You are going to do this for four years, so you are going to need regular maintenance such as oil changes, along with some major expenses such as a new set of tires. You are also going to need a reliable car to begin with. If your car breaks down during finals week, you are going to have to do a lot of explaining to your professors, who will not be very sympathetic.

With these words of caution in mind, commuting might still be the best option for you. Not everyone lives down the street from their dream school, but most people live within driving distance of at least one college, and it still ends up being less expensive than living on your own.

Online Options

One way to avoid the commute to school is to take online classes. The number of options has exploded in recent years. They were originally designed for nontraditional students because students who had full-time jobs and a family needed greater flexibility. Some courses require at least some contact with the professor in a classroom setting, usually at the beginning of the term. Thereafter, students do most of the work on their own, checking in with the professor and their class through an online chat room. Work can be assigned and turned in through the internet. Testing varies. In some cases, exams have to be proctored by an approved person, while other courses require a trip to a real classroom.

If you are interested in completing much of your coursework this way, be sure to check out all of the curriculum requirements thoroughly to make sure that you are not going to run into any problems. These should be listed on the course website, and you can always check with the professor to be sure. If you have research projects, you could end up spending so much time driving to the library or the lab that you might as well have taken class on campus. Your local public library cannot compete with a college library that caters to students by subscribing to specialized journals and ordering books and other research materials.

You also need to make sure that you have the motivation to get the work done on time without a great deal of prompting. Some students need teacher interaction to learn. Your ability to succeed in an online course may depend on the subject matter. If you usually have trouble with English or math, you may be better off in the classroom.

Books

Books are a tremendous expense for students to incur on top of all the other expenses, such as fees and housing. Some of the instructors have written the textbooks, so there is that to consider as well. Plus, every year it seems there is a new edition, driving students to always have to purchase the latest copy and hence doing away with the ability to make purchases of used books. Plus, books often have CD-ROMs or access codes that are enclosed with the books, just to drive up the cost even more.

Do we need all those expensive textbooks? Probably not, now that the internet and eBooks are so available. Hopefully someday some of the demand for buying textbooks for college classes will be limited or eliminated, but until then, we need to make the best of it and get the books as cheaply as possible.

Five ways to save on textbooks now:

- **Buy or rent textbooks online:** There are hundreds of sites where students can buy, sell, and even rent textbooks for a fraction of the cost. Some basics include **www.amazon. com**, **www.campusbooks.com**, and **www.ebay.com**. To find other good websites, here are some keywords to search:

"used textbooks," "[your school] bookswap," "textbook price comparison," or any ISBN.

- **Shop overseas:** Many American textbooks are available at a fraction of their cost through overseas websites. Check out foreign versions of leading American websites like **www. amazon.co.uk** or get overseas prices for Thomson Learning books by going directly to their website and clicking another country at the main page. Shipping can often take several weeks, so make sure to leave enough time. Also, foreign editions may have minor differences, so as a rule of thumb, make sure the ISBN matches. make sure the ISBN matches.

- **Swap:** There are many ways to find used books to buy, borrow, or trade just by contacting other students:

  - Ask around: Ask your friends, your friends' roommates, etc. It is not hard to find someone who has taken the class before, and you will save on shipping, too.

  - Facebook (and other social media): Look for used book groups, and search for people who have taken the class before. Try Craigslist also.

  - Bookswaps: Use nonprofit government's website.

- **Check it out:** School libraries often stock copies of commonly used textbooks. If you get there early you might be lucky enough to check one out, but at the very least, instructors will typically put one copy on reserve at the library for everyone to access. If you cannot get a book for free, you might still save money by renting. There are several online rental programs that might have the book you need, and several colleges and communities have locally based programs.

- **Do your homework:** Ask professors if you can use an older edition or a version without any "bundled" items like CDs. To make the search easier, ask your instructor for the ISBN number, which is the unique code for each book.

Here are a few other good sites to buy, sell, and rent used textbooks:

- **www.textbooks.com**
- **www.bigwords.com**
- **www.iCollegeWeb.com**
- **www.chegg.com** (and you can rent, buy and sell them)
- **www.ebay.com**
- **www.amazon.com**

These sites offer long-term solutions for lowering the prices, as well as recent news about what is happening in the legal sector regarding lowering the cost of textbooks.

What is so great about buying online?

- It is fast and easy.
- You save money buying used textbooks.
- You can generally find the textbooks you need.
- You can rent textbooks at a cheaper cost.

Keep in mind that you will also incur shipping expenses when purchasing online. Remember that you will need to save the box they came in for return if renting or if you want to sell them back.

Chapter 7

Work It Out

ven with grants, scholarships, and loans, sometimes it is a good idea to supplement your college years with extra work. Working off some of your college costs can reduce your need for more loans. Remember, loans are money that you must start paying back generally six months after graduation. Consider the fact that working while you're in college drastically limits your financial aid. Weigh the pros and cons of working while you're taking classes because your newfound income can affect your entire college experience.

If you decide that a job doesn't affect your financial aid too drastically, then you need to find a job that compensates for the slight dip in government help.

Let us look at some of the opportunities you can exploit to work your way through college.

Identify Your Resources

Your education and professional training are not your only personal resources. What other experience have you gained during your life? What are your talents and hobbies? Are you outgoing and a good public speaker? Are you an introverted writer? You may be able to put your abilities to work to increase your earning power.

An artist can put some of his or her work up for sale in a gallery or rent a space at a weekend art festival. A good cook can cater for parties or decorate birthday cakes. A musician can accompany performers at local clubs. Even if activities like these are not immediately lucrative, it is important to start them, gain experience, and give them time to develop.

Your computer can be used to enhance your income in many ways, whether you use it to do work, advertise a business, sell something, network with colleagues, or conduct research.

CASE STUDY:
Lisa McGinnes

Being able to graduate from college debt-free was an enormous help to me, since I would choose a career as a journalist and would then work in the nonprofit sector, where the pay is never very high. Not having student loan payments probably allowed me to live in my own apartment without a roommate, and to buy my first new car at the age of 23.

It wasn't easy, though. I would have liked to attend a more prestigious college out of state, but ended up selecting a state school that offered me an academic scholarship that covered my entire tuition and some books. I knew in high school that I needed to keep my grades up, and I received a few small scholarships from organizations like the local Kiwanis club that also helped cover expenses. Luckily for me, my dad was willing to work a lot of overtime shifts to pay my room and board fees.

After my freshman year, I worked a part-time job on campus to earn spending money. I also wrote for the college newspaper, which gave me experience and a little more cash. If I had the time and needed to make bank, my side hustle was typing and editing research papers for other students. My best client was an athlete majoring in P.E. He couldn't type and wasn't a particularly good writer. He often waited until the last minute and was willing to pay double my normal fees for a "rush" job. I think he pretty much supplied all my pizza money!

Lisa McGinnes is now a writer and magazine editor. She earned a bachelor's degree in public relations from Western Michigan University.

Work Part-Time

If you are looking to land work during college, you might want to check the college's student employment office. Another good source is to check **www.Monster.com**, **www.CareerBuilder.com**, and **www.Indeed.com**. Temporary work and even long-term opportunities can be found through temporary agencies. Although temp agencies may specialize in temporary work, they offer permanent jobs as well. Some of the temp agencies allow you to apply for work online, although an initial interview may be required. Just remember that many of these agencies charge you a fee to find you a job that you might be able to get for yourself first, so resort to these as a last choice.

Many businesses advertise for help with "Help Wanted" signs in their windows, while other, larger companies have ongoing needs for new employees year-round. Many times, if you have a part-time job in in your hometown and that business is also in your college town, they will transfer you when you start college. Some jobs will be better preparations for after graduation, so you might want to consider trying to find any work you can in your field. A foot in the door can really lead to that door opening to future opportunities for you.

Getting early experience in your career helps you out in many ways, such as:

- Earning money even with part-time jobs.

- Resume building: You are gaining some work experience, which is good for your resume.

- Getting your feet wet: You may be learning about your field before you finish school.

- Career choice: You may find that there are other career choices in your field and find one that might suit you even better than the one you had planned.

- Networking: You may be making contacts that will help later in your job search.

- Learning skills: You are learning new skills such as knowing how to work as a team and learning how to do a specific task.

When looking for a job, and even after you have found one, remember to:

- Keep your résumé up-to-date.

- Start to build a network: Get names and numbers of those whom you might contact later.

- Get your letters of recommendation: It is easier to get them now, rather than backtrack.

- If applicable, start to build your portfolio: Make sure you get copies of what you have worked on.

To find a job, try the following:

- Check the want ads.

- Ask at your school's career center.

- Look at bulletin boards.

- Go to job fairs.

- Ask friends, family, and fellow students if they have heard of anything available.

- Make cold calls: Either call businesses or stop in and fill out an application.

- Sign up at temp agencies: Sometimes temp jobs turn into longer jobs.

- Register with an agency in person and/or online.

Cooperative Education

Cooperative education combines secondary education with work experience that is practical for the focus of your studies. Often the programs are designed to have you alternate semesters of academic study with semesters of full-time employment in positions related to your academic or career interests, although there are other situations. Some colleges offer programs with cooperative education. For instance, NC State University, the largest university in North Carolina, has 10 colleges with most major academic disciplines, as well as graduate school with programs in over 100 areas.

Some of the benefits with receiving a cooperative education are:

- Practical experience in your field of study.
- Your education is applied to real-life work situations.
- You make useful contacts.

- You learn real-life working skills.
- You earn money.

A great source of information about cooperative education is with the National Commission for Cooperative Education (NCCE). Since 1962, the Commission and its college and business partners have supported the development of quality work-integrated learning programs through: National Advocacy, Executive Outreach, Public Awareness, Students & Parent Response Center, and Research & Education.

The Commission developed a co-op model to define what cooperative education should consist of. The characteristics for this model, as detailed on their website, are: formal recognition by the school, structure for multiple work experiences, work experiences related to career or academic goals, and provision for employer and school evaluations.

You can find out more about the Commission at **www.co-op.edu**.

Paid Internships

One way to gain work experience in your field of study and perhaps receive academic is with internships. Internships are approved and monitored work experience related to your field of study that meet learning goals. Some internships can help you receive academic credit for your internship, but you generally have to get the internship approved beforehand by your school. Some schools have an office that is in charge of helping to find internships for students. However, even if you school does not offer academic credit for internships or assist you with finding an internship, they may be worth pursuing on your own. Some of the benefits of internships include:

- You will gain a deeper understanding about a career.
- You will have work experience in your field once you graduate.
- You will be able to find out if you are pursuing the right career.
- You will learn valuable skills.
- You will make connections and start to network.
- If you are planning to go to graduate school, you have an extra edge on your application.
- Many internships not only pay, but some pay rather well.

Before you find out how to get an internship, you might first try to decide what kind interests you and what you hope to gain from it. Figure out what kind of company you would like to work for. Ask yourself if you will only take a paid internship or if you are willing to work in an unpaid position. Also think about how long of an internship you are interested in.

Once you have pondered what you want from an internship, you have to find one. You might first ask your school adviser or department head if they know where to look. There may be plenty of resources at your school to help you find an internship, such as a bulletin board with a listing, their website, or an internship adviser on staff. Perhaps your uncle works for a company you are interested in interning at. Why not give him a call?

You can always research the company you are interested in and see if they have something posted on their website about internships and who to contact. You might also try local career fairs, as some companies have information about internships available at fairs and other recruitment events.

Work Study

If you are interested in working while in school, you can apply for programs at your school that are designed to enhance your education.

The Federal Work-Study Program (FWS) was formerly known as the College Work-Study Program. According to the U.S. Department of Education:

> The FWS Program provides funds that are earned through part-time employment to assist students in financing the costs of postsecondary financial aid administrators at participating institutions have substantial flexibility in determining the amount of FWS awards to provide to students who are enrolled or accepted for enrollment. Hourly wages must not be less than the federal minimum wage.

The Federal Work-Study Program (FWS) helps you contribute to your acquired skills and learning new skills while employed either on campus or in a community service role.

Generally, the process to apply for a work-study program is to complete the FAFSA, and then complete an application at your school should they offer this program. You must meet the financial requirements according to FAFSA and maintain academic success, as defined by your school, to participate in this program while you attend school. Another advantage of the Work-Study Program is that it often pays more than minimum-wage jobs.

Ask your academic adviser if there are work-study opportunities at your school, as it is great way to earn campus.

AmeriCorps & National Service

Take advantage of an opportunity to work for AmeriCorps and you could earn a Segal AmeriCorps Education Award equivalent to the maximum value of the Pell Grant ($5,815 as of Oct. 2015-which can change year to year) to student loans[10] AmeriCorps works in partnership with nonprofits, state and local agencies, and faith-based agencies to complete service projects throughout the region. While you work for AmeriCorps you are helping those across the country in community service positions. According to AmeriCorps, the positions range from the chance to:

- Tutor and mentor disadvantaged youth
- Fight illiteracy
- Improve health services
- Build affordable housing
- Teach computer skills
- Clean parks and streams
- Manage or operate after-school programs
- Help communities respond to disasters
- Build organizational capacity
- Get college credit for two classes – Intro to Service Learning and Diversity in Service.

You are paid a "modest living allowance during service (around $91 a week), and once you complete your service you can apply for the Segal AmeriCorps Education Award."

There are several programs that you can apply for, including the AmeriCorps State and National that offers national projects like residential programs for men and women age 18 to 24.

---

10. Corporation for National and Community Service, 2017

You can apply for AmeriCorps and find out more about the Segal Ameri-iCorps Education Award and other Corps as well at **www.national service.gov/programs/americorps**.

Reserves, National Guard & R.O.T.C

If you have thought about joining the National Guard or the Reserves, you may be pleased to hear about their program College First, which is designed to allow you to attend undergraduate or graduate school full-time, all while earning over $2,000 per month, with a guarantee of no deployment during your first two years of Guard service. According to the National Guard, "The program also includes many financial benefits that could potentially pay for your entire education."

The National Guard states that you are eligible if: you have no experience in the military, have graduated high school, and meet all other National Guard Enlistment Standards. You can receive an enlistment bonus of $20,000, 100-percent tuition assistance, the MGIB-SR Kicker (an extra $350 per month of educational assistance), the Montgomery G.I. Bill (an extra $317 per month of educational assistance), and up to two years of nondeployment following completion of Initial Active Duty Training (IADT).

> * *Recruiting Assistant Pay (Voluntary): This is a 100 percent optional, performance-based program open to Guard members to assist in helping recruit for your unit. Recruiting Assistants (RAs) can earn additional income assisting Guard recruiting efforts, by identifying well-qualified men and women for service in the ARNG. RAs earn $2,000 for each new recruit who enlists and reports to Basic Training or for each prior service member who affiliates with a unit for four months. Monthly dollar amount is based on one referral enlisting each quarter.*

The Army National Guard funds up to 100 percent of tuition costs and fees, not to exceed $250 per semester hour and will be limited to $4,500 per person per fiscal year.

Contact your local recruiter for details about College First in your **www.1800goguard.com** to find out more about the Reserves or the National Guard and what college benefits are available to you.

There are also ROTC scholarships available at specific colleges. These vary in amounts, some paying stipends along with up to 100 percent tuition. Of course, there are requirements and stipulations. Your best course of action would be to contact the colleges and recruiters.

Freelancing

Freelancing is doing one-time projects or consultations for a fee. It is not steady employment like a regular job, but it provides opportunities for you to use your talents to earn extra income. Freelancing might involve creating a website for a small business, photographing a family reunion, setting up a home computer for a neighbor, writing a magazine article, or preparing someone's taxes.

Freelancing can broaden your network of contacts and add to your work experience. You may be able to experiment with a new type of career or start a business of your own without losing the security of your primary employment. Just be careful to not overwork yourself that you neglect your schooling.

Wrapping It Up

A great way to lower your college costs is by working off some of the costs, though you may change the amount of financial aid you receive. There are plenty of ways you can do so, including work-study opportunities, internships, and cooperative education. If you are inclined to join the National Guard, or Reserves, you might find that they offer several ways to help you pay for college. Paying for college along the way can lead to lower student loans and bills that you will be responsible to pay for upon graduation. Plus, working your way through college helps pay your personal expenses while you attend school.

No matter what job or what program you are working for, keep in mind the following tips while you work.

- Be on time for work.

- Do not leave early or take long lunches, unless approved by your supervisor.

- Do not bad-mouth others that you work with. The grapevine leaves a nasty trail.

- Accept constructive criticism rather than getting angry about it.

- Ask for feedback, especially if you do not receive a formal review.

- Be a team player.

- Always put your best foot forward

Chapter 8

Loans as a Last Resort

mericans owe more than $1.4 trillion in student loan debt, with about 44 million borrowers carrying that incredible burden. The average 2016 graduate has over $37,000 in debt entering the workforce.[11]

Although the focus of this book is graduating debt-free, if you can't quite make that happen, student loans can be a valuable financial tool. Student loans are available to students of all ages, but they are particularly significant for young high school graduates who are ready to enter college but do not have financial resources to do so. Loans should be treated as a last option since they linger long after you've graduated college.

---

11. Student Loan Hero, 2017

First, consider asking family members for financial help. If your mom, dad, or great aunt can lend you money, it'll be better for you in the long run. You can work out a payment plan that doesn't include interest – which costs you more when taking out a federal loan.

When you apply for student loans, there are likely many things going through your mind besides how you could pay them off or what being in debt might mean for your future. You are likely just excited and relieved that your application can be approved, and you are probably preoccupied with registering for the right classes and finding a place to live.

A student loan is a serious debt obligation. If you manage it poorly, you may end up adding thousands of dollars to your debt, and the damage to your credit rating will have a negative effect on many aspects of your life, including your eligibility for certain jobs, how much you can pay for a mortgage, your car payments, and your ability to achieve financial freedom.

What is a Student Loan?

A student loan is money that is borrowed to pay for school tuition, room and board, and other expenses gained while studying at an institution of higher learning. Unlike scholarships and grants, student loans must be paid back with interest.

Loans work like this:

1. You choose the type of loan and how much you wish to borrow.

2. The date the loan is borrowed – or issued – begins the start of interest building on your loan.

3. The bank or lending system decides the interest rate you will pay on top of the borrowed money.

4. Depending on the type, some loans don't need to be paid off until after you've graduated college. Some loans, once you make the first payment, will then start the payment schedule. Check to see what type of payment plan or schedule loans have before deciding on one.

Fast Fact ▨▨▨▨▨▨▨▨▨▨▨▨▨▨▨▨▨▨▨▨▨▨▨▨▨▨▨▨▨▨▨▨▨▨▨

Interest - otherwise known as an interest rate - is the amount of extra money due on the amount loaned to a person. For example, if a loan of $10,000 is borrowed on January 1, 2018 at an interest rate of four percent, to be paid out over the next five years, then the monthly payment would be $185 dollars, and the loan would be paid off by January 1, 2023. The quicker you pay off a loan, the less interest will build up against you. In fact, putting an extra $20 on the principal each month cuts down the payment schedule by 6 months - making the payment complete by July 1, 2022. Try it for yourself at **www. bankrate.com/calculators.aspx**

The three major types of student loans are guaranteed and sometimes subsidized by the government; they include Stafford, Perkins, and PLUS loans, which are taken out and repaid by the student's family. Banks also offer private student loans. Consolidation loans enable a borrower to pay off several individual loans and assume a single monthly payment. Peer-to-peer loans are a recent innovation in which a student signs a formal loan contract to borrow money from a friend or family member for education expenses.

Unfortunately, about half of the freshmen who enter postsecondary institutions in the United States do not graduate with a degree. So, figuring out a way to remain debt-free is crucial for success.

Anatomy of a Student Loan

The federal student loan program is intended to help students pay for higher education by lending them money at interest rates lower than commercial interest rates, with flexible repayment plans that make student loans manageable for young graduates entering the work force.

In an ordinary market, a high school graduate with little or no credit history would not be able to qualify for a loan from a commercial lender, or would be charged extremely high interest rates to compensate for the risk. The federal government makes low-interest student loans possible by transferring that risk to itself, and by giving lenders a guaranteed rate of return.

The major federal loan programs – Stafford (both Subsidized and Unsubsidized), PLUS, Grad PLUS, and Consolidation – are administered in two ways, the Direct Loan program and the FFEL program. Each college or university decides which program will provide federally guaranteed loans to its students.

The government itself is the lender under the Direct Loan program. The U.S. government borrows money from the U.S. Treasury and disburses it directly to student borrowers through their school financial aid offices. Students repay the loans directly to the government. The Direct Loan program is administered by the U.S. Department of Education, but the federal government hires private contractors to do most of the work of servicing the loans and collecting the defaulted loans.

How to Get a Student Loan

The first step in applying for a student loan is to fill out a FAFSA. On the application, list the schools to which you have applied. Based on your FAFSA, the Department of Education will prepare for the Student Aid Report (SAR), which the schools will use to determine how much you are eligible to receive in Perkins and Subsidized and Unsubsidized Stafford Loans.

The school will also offer PLUS loans to make up the difference between its Cost of Attendance and the amount available in financial aid. The school will ask you to sign a Master Promissory Note, and the federal loan funds will be disbursed through the school financial aid office. Loans are disbursed in at least two installments, none of which can exceed half of the total amount of the loan.

The funds will be applied to tuition, fees, room and board, and other charges payable to the school, and a check will be issued to the student for the remaining balance of the loan.

Parents may not qualify for PLUS loans because they are not creditworthy, or they may not be able to immediately begin making the required monthly loans. If you are short of necessary funds, you can apply for private student loans.

Who Gets Government Loans?

Government student loans are guaranteed and subsidized by the U.S. Government. They are typically arranged and disbursed through the school's financial aid office and the funds are applied directly to qualified educational expenses such as tuition, fees, and dormitory costs. Subsidized loans, in which the government pays the interest while the student is in school or in deferment, are based on some students demonstrated financial need. Unsubsidized loans are available to any student, regardless of need.

There is a limit to the amount that can be borrowed each academic term. You cannot qualify for a government loan if you are not a United States citizen or qualified non-citizen (such as a Green Card holder), have a drug conviction, or are eligible but have not registered for Selective Service.

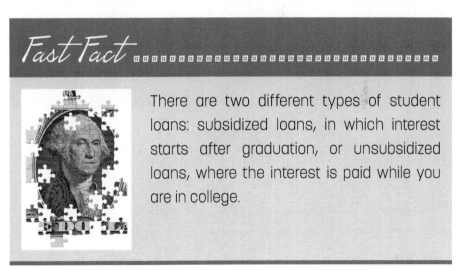

Fast Fact ▫▫▫▫▫▫▫▫▫▫▫▫▫▫▫▫▫▫▫▫▫▫▫▫▫▫▫▫▫▫▫▫▫▫▫▫▫▫

There are two different types of student loans: subsidized loans, in which interest starts after graduation, or unsubsidized loans, where the interest is paid while you are in college.

Stafford Loans

Stafford student loans are the most common type of government loan. They are low-interest loans made to undergraduates who attend an accredited college or university as full- or half-time students. Loan payments are deferred while you are in school. The government pays the interest on subsidized Stafford loans during your in-school deferment, but you are responsible for paying the interest that accrues on unsubsidized loans while you are in school. You can either begin making interest payments while you are in school, or allow the interest to be added to the principal balance of the loan when your deferment ends, increasing the size and cost of the loan.

There are two types of Stafford Loans – Federal Family Educational Loans (FFEL) and Direct Loans. Private lenders, such as banks, credit unions, savings and loans, and non-profit lenders fund FFEL program loans, which are guaranteed against default by the federal government.

The amount of subsidized Stafford loans you receive is based on financial need and is determined once you have submitted your FAFSA. Every student is eligible for unsubsidized Stafford loans, but there is a limit on the total amount of Stafford loans a student can receive while studying for a degree.

Perkins Loans

Perkins Loans are low-interest loans awarded by the school to undergraduate and graduate students with exceptional financial need. The federal government sets aside a limited pool of money to fund these loans, and the school is expected to contribute an amount that is equal to at least one-third of the amount provided by the government.

A Perkins Loan offers better terms and benefits than any other student loan. It is a subsidized loan, meaning that the interest is paid by the federal government during the in-school deferment and grace period, which is nine months after graduation instead of the usual six months. Perkins Loans have no origination or default fees. The interest rate is five percent, and the loan has a 10-year repayment period.

PLUS Loans

Parental Loans for Undergraduate Students (PLUS) are designed to help parents meet the Expected Family Contribution (EFC) for a dependent undergraduate student enrolled at least half time in an eligible program at an eligible school. Like Stafford loans, PLUS loans are available from lending institutions through the Federal Family Education Loan (FFEL) Program. Parents with an acceptable credit history qualify for a PLUS loan.

The limit on a PLUS Loan is equal to the student's cost of attendance minus any other financial aid received. Any money remaining after tuition, fees, and other charges have been paid is disbursed to the parents and must be used for education expenses. PLUS loans are guaranteed by the federal government. Parents are charged a fee of up to four percent of the loan amount, deducted from the disbursement.

Private Loans

Private loans are not subsidized or guaranteed by the federal government, nor are they subject to the same regulation. Private loans are used to make up the difference between financial aid and federal loans, or students' and families expected contribution.

Most of the lenders in the federal loan program also sell private loans. Some lenders originally developed private loans to provide supplements to their student borrowers of federal loans and to satisfy school requirements for "preferred lenders." To make private student loan pools more attractive, most private lenders charge borrowers guarantee fees and purchase insurance with companies such as The Education Resource Institute (TERI) – the oldest and largest private, nonprofit guarantor of private student loans – that ensure that principal and accrued interest will be paid to the lender if the loan goes into default.

Private loans versus federal loans

Private loans are issued by individual banks that set their own lending policies and are not governed by federal guidelines. Private loans are not included in federal loan-cancellation programs, which means that private loan holders do not have the same freedom to enter low-paid public service careers. Though they charge higher interest rates than federal student loans, private student loans are similarly protected from discharge during bankruptcy.

Fast Fact ▪▫

The Public Service Loan Forgiveness (PSLF) Program forgives the balance of your loan once you've made 120 consecutive qualifying payments on it under a qualifying repayment plan while working full-time for a qualifying business.[12]

Protection

Federal loans offer protections for borrowers, including income-based repayment, deferment, forbearance, and cancellation rights. Private lenders may offer some of these options, but they are not required to. When the lender does offer these options, the details are often not spelled out in the loan document. If a student borrower dies or becomes permanently disabled, a federal loan can be cancelled, but the student's family will still be responsible for paying off private student loans.

Interest rates

The underlying difference between federal and private loans is that federal loans are structured to benefit the student, while private loans are structured to benefit the lenders and investors – no surprise there. All federal loans have interest-rate caps – in most cases, with fixed rates set at 6.8 percent (8.5 for PLUS loans). Nearly all private loans have vari-

---

12. U.S. Department of Education, 2017

able interest rates with no upper limits, and some have "floors" that limit how low the interest rate can drop.

Many private loans are quite expensive, with interest rates of up to 15 percent or higher. The variable rate is often set at the market prime rate plus a "margin" based on the borrower's credit rating. This margin can be as much as 10 percent.

Cost

Private loans are almost always more expensive than federal loans. Except for PLUS loans, borrowers of federal loans are not required to be creditworthy; it is assumed that students have artificially low credit scores because they have little or no credit history. What 18-year-old has history renting an apartment, having a mortgage, or purchasing a vehicle? Not that many.

Most private loans are priced according to creditworthiness. A student without a creditworthy cosigner will be charged a higher interest rate because of his or her limited credit history. Some lenders base their rates on the school that a student is attending, charging a higher interest rate for schools with a higher default rate.

How Much Can I Borrow?

When it comes to the Stafford program, your college will first decide how much tuition, books, and room and board costs. Once total costs are finalized, FAFSA and your expected family contribution will kick in. The maximum amount an undergraduate can borrow through a Stafford loan is $5,500[13] If a student is financially dependent, then the rate can

---

13. U.S. News, 2010

change. For the first year, students can borrow $5,500. The second year, he or she can borrow $6,500. For the third year until graduation, he or she can borrow $7,500 yearly.

Student Loan Forgiveness

If you have no choice but to take out student loans, there are several career tracks that will allow you to have your loans "forgiven" or cancelled before you have paid in full.

Public service

Your student loans may be eligible for forgiveness after you make 120 qualifying payments while working for a qualifying employer.[14] Basically means that you make your complete monthly payment on time

---

14. U.S. Department of Education, 2017

every month for 10 years while employed by one of the following types of organizations:

- Government organizations – federal, state, local, or tribal (this includes public school teachers, firefighters, and law enforcement officers)

- Tax exempt, 501 (c)(3) nonprofit organizations

- Americorps or Peace Corps

Of course there are many more specifics on loan forgiveness – only direct loans are eligible, but Perkins Loans may be able to be consolidated into a forgiveness-eligible loan. If you are considering a career in law enforcement, teaching, or other government or nonprofit jobs, this might be a great option for you, considering the average bachelor's degree holder takes 21 years to pay off their student loans.[15] Much more information is available at **https://studentaid.ed.gov**.

Armed Forces

If you choose a career in the military, a portion of your student loans may be eligible for forgiveness through your branch of service: Army, Navy, Air Force, or National Guard. Check with the service branch for details on qualifying loans and careers:

- **www.goarmy.com**
- **www.navy.com**
- **www.airforce.com**
- **www.nationalguard.com**

---

15. U.S. News, 2014

Health care

If you choose a career in healthcare, including professions like nursing, physican, dentistry, or pharmacy, you may qualify for loan forgiveness.

For more information on qualifying employment for student loan forgiveness, refer to **https://studentaid.ed.gov**.

Interest and Payment Plans

Federal education loans offer four main repayment plans. The repayment options for a private loan are defined in the loan contract and vary from lender to lender. The type of payment plan that is best for you depends on your financial situation when you graduate. For instance, if your degree is in accounting, you won't necessarily start a career in a low-paying job. On the other hand, if you chose a degree in philosophy, the jobs available to you fresh out of college aren't high-paying. You might have to work your way up to a job that adequately pays the bills.

For that reason, be aware of your loan terms. If you suddenly come into a large sum of money, you can choose to pay off your loan. Private lenders impose a penalty for early payment, but – face it – how often is it that you win huge stacks of cash from the lottery or the trust fund promised to you at twenty-five is suddenly available now? It's unlikely that a loan could be dealt with earlier than the deadline, but bear in mind the penalty in case you're fortunate enough to do so.

Let's talk about repayment plans that set you up for success.

Federal student loans - standard repayment plan

Under a standard repayment plan, you make a fixed monthly payment for a term of up to 10 years. If your loan was not a large one, the term may be shorter, but most college graduates need at least ten years to pay off their loans. Think about that! This means that each month a minimum of $50 must go toward your student loans *for the next ten years.* That's the cost equivalent to a monthly cell phone bill, dinner at a fancy restaurant, Netflix and Hulu with snacks for several weeks, or even – have mercy! – internet for one month!

Some or most of these things are a necessity to every millennial, so, let's face it – avoiding student loans makes your life that much sweeter. Imagine going without internet every month to afford your student loans. Not a pretty picture.

If you can't avoid loans, try to find a job right before you graduate from college. Having a job lined up can help you avoid needing to cut back on simple pleasures. Finding a well-paying job shortly before leaving college is the best option for success. It doesn't have to be in your career field of choice, but not falling behind on student loan payments will save you major heartache because your credit won't suffer.

Since standard repayment plans offer the best interest rate of all repayment plans, this loan option is the best way to go – if you can't avoid taking out a loan.

Federal student loans - extended repayment plan

Under an extended repayment plan, fixed loan payments are stretched out over a longer term of 12 to 30 years, depending on the amount of the loan. The size of each payment is reduced, but the additional interest you will pay over the extended term will increase the total amount repaid over the lifetime of a loan. The smaller monthly payments are easier to manage when your income is low, you have many monthly bills and obligations, or you have had financial setbacks. All these reasons add up to getting an extended repayment plan. The minimum monthly payment is $50.

Consider this: most home mortgages come with 30 year loans. Do you really want to pay the equivalent of a mortgage on a college education? Life comes with financial setbacks, so be certain you can't pay off a loan quicker before you choose this option. The extra years it takes to pay off an extended loan can cost you an extra several thousand dollars over the course of 30 years.

If your chosen career is in a sector with very low starting salaries, like public service, you may be eligible for other types of repayment that start with smaller monthly payment and increase as your salary goes up. Read more info at **www.finaid.org.**

Repayment options for private loans

Private lenders are not required to offer the same repayment options as federal loans. Repayment options vary from lender to lender. Most lenders offer some form of extended payment plans, deferment, and forbearance, but the requirements may be different or they may charge additional fees. Review your private loan contracts carefully to understand what rights you have. If you are in danger of default because of financial difficulties, some lenders may offer options that are not specifically spelled out in the loan contract; you will not know until you ask.

What Plan is Best for You?

You will pay the least for your loans, and become debt free most quickly, if you opt for the Standard Repayment Plan and pay off the entire loan in ten years or less. Your financial realities, though, may make it necessary to choose a different repayment plan. Most financial advisors recommend that your student loan payment be between 10 and 15 percent of your annual gross income (AGI). Any more than that and you are likely to encounter financial hardships and have difficulty making your payments.

If your monthly loan payment under a Standard Repayment Plan exceeds 15 percent of your annual gross income, you should consider changing to a payment plan that allows you to make lower monthly payments, at least until your financial circumstances improve. You can still make additional loan payments whenever you have some extra cash.

Student loan repayment calculators on Finaid.org (**www.finaid.org/ calculators/scripts/loanpayments.cgi**) and CollegeBoard.com (**apps.**

collegeboard.com/fincalc/sla.jsp) help estimate what your monthly loan payment will be under a Standard Repayment Plan.

Managing Your Loan Payments

Lowering your interest rate

A half of one percent may seem like a small number, but when you are calculating interest over a repayment period of ten or twenty years, it can add up to a considerable sum of money. You will want to consider any option that will lower your interest rate because it means big savings in the long run.

Many lenders offer interest rate reductions – typically 0.25 percent – if you sign up for automatic payments from your checking account or for electronic billing. Lenders also offer interest rate reductions as reward for making payments on time, for example, a one-percent reduction after you make the first 24 or 36 consecutive payments on time, for as long as you continue to be on time. You will lose this reduction if a single payment is late, and until now, only 10 percent of borrowers have been able to retain it.

Temporary solutions

Student loans offer a number of features not available with other types of loans, designed to help a borrower avoid default and keep up regular loan payments.

Depending on your circumstances, deferment, forbearance, or loan consolidation may be short-term solutions if you are having trouble making your loan payments.

Deferment

Certain conditions qualify you for a loan deferment on federally guaranteed loans, a period during which student loan payments are suspended. The interest on loans in deferment is lower than the interest on repayment or forbearance. Interest on government subsidized loans is paid by the government during deferment periods. The interest that grows on unsubsidized loans during the deferment period will be added to the loan balance – or capitalized – and increase the total amount that you will repay in the long run, so it is wise to make at least the interest payments if possible. You do not jeopardize your deferment status if you make payments on a loan during a period of deferment.

If you have already defaulted on your loans, you are not eligible for deferment.

If you meet all the eligibility requirements, your lender cannot deny deferment. You must complete necessary paperwork and submit it to your lender using the most recent version of the application form; because deferment is offered through the federal government, your lender cannot accept outdated or incomplete forms. Deferment forms for Direct Loans are available on the Federal Student Aid website at **www.dl.ed.gov** and for other federally-guaranteed loans on **www. Salliemae.com**.

Some conditions that qualify you for deferment include:

- Enrolling in graduate school
- Participating in rehabilitation training
- Receiving state unemployment benefits
- Serving in active-duty military service

Forbearance

If you do not qualify for deferments, or you have private student loans, you can request forbearance from your lender. Forbearance is permission to temporarily delay loan payments during a period of financial difficulty. It can also involve granting an extension to your payment period or approving lower payments. You might need to request forbearance if you are ineligible for in-school deferment because you are attending classes less than half-time; if poor health impacts your ability to work or make payments; if you have exceeded the deferment period for unemployment; if your work hours are suddenly reduced; or if you experience a life-changing event, such as the birth of a baby or the death of a spouse.

Consolidation

Consolidating a loan is something life refinancing a loan. Your lender pays off one or more of your existing loans and gives you a single new loan with a fixed interest rate. The advantages are that you will have only one loan payment to manage, you may be able to extend your payment period and lower the amount of your monthly payment – though you will end up paying more over the life of the loan if you take longer to pay it off – and you may be able to lock in a lower interest rate. You can also use a loan consolidation to become eligible for certain programs, such as the income-contingent repayment plan that is offered only through Direct Loans.

Adjusting your payment

According to Sallie Mae, financial experts recommend that your student loan payment should be no more than 10 percent of your monthly income before taxes. When a loan payment consumes too much of your monthly income, it can seriously impact other important financial priorities. If your scheduled monthly loan payment is too high to be sustainable on your current income, lower your payment by switching to another payment plan.

Lenders often use your debt-to-income ratio – the percentage of your monthly income that is spent on paying off debt – to determine whether you can take on additional debt. To calculate your debt-to-income, add up all your monthly debt payments, including your student loans, credit card payments, car payments, rent, and divide them by your total monthly income. A debt-to-income ratio of 10 percent or less is considered excellent. If your debt-to-income ratio exceeds 21 percent, your resources are overextended. If the ratio is 36 percent or higher, you are in serious financial danger. If your debt-to-income ratio approaches 20 percent, it is a sign that you should seek a lower monthly student loan payment.

Because you can change repayment plans once a year, you should revisit your repayment plan regularly, especially if your financial circumstances change because of a new job or a layoff, marriage or divorce, inheritance, or business success. Whatever plan you choose, you can always make extra payments to reduce the loan balance.

The Dangers of Not Paying on Time

A student loan payment is technically delinquent the day after the due date. If you miss one payment, a lender may consider you to be late 30 days even though you believe you are only one day late.

After you miss a second payment on a government loan, the Department of Education requires the lender to notify the guarantor that you are delinquent and in danger of defaulting on the loan. These procedures are required by law, and neither the lender nor the guarantor can deviate from them.

A government loan (FFEL) scheduled for regular monthly payments can go into default after you have missed payments for 270 days – or 9 months – according to current law. If payments are scheduled less frequently, the loan goes into default after 330 days. Private loans may have different criteria for determining when the loan is in default.

Consequences of default

The consequences of default on a student loan are serious. If you default on a government loan, and the guarantor is unable to rehabilitate the loan, the guarantor must immediately pay the lender the principal and all the interest due on the loan. The guarantor seeks reimbursement from the government, and the government takes over the job of recovering the loss from you, the borrower.

This means the government can take your income tax refunds to pay your debt, and can take legal action against you including garnishing your wages. They also have the right to collect legal fees and collection agency fees from you.

If your student loan is in default, you may not be eligible to receive financial aid or additional student loans if you decide to return to school to continue your education or get a professional degree. This can be especially harmful if you dropped out of school after one or two years and now wish to return and complete your first degree.

Defaulted student loans can keep you from being eligible for some types of mortgages, and will drastically lower your credit score, which will harm you financially with everything from car loans to rent applications.

One a student loan enters default, rehabilitation is a complicated process, and some of the harmful consequences cannot be reversed. Make use of every option available, including reducing payments and forbearance to avoid default.

Chapter 9

Live Dangerously –
Graduate Debt-Free!

et's talk about some of the dangers you might face on the path to financial freedom. Some troubles might confront you as you try to avoid large loans, splurging too much, and living large. Students who try their hardest to remain debt-free could face scholarship scams, credit card debt, financial aid issues, or even bankruptcy or default on loans. Some people find themselves in these predicaments even though they worked hard to avoid trouble.

When it comes to college funding, sometimes it is easy to lose sight of your goal, "Get your degree while going into the least amount of debt." You may try to fool yourself into thinking that you can pay the money back someday, or why should you worry about the money now when you have school to think about. You need to think about whether or not the payments will be so steep that you will not be able to afford rent (yes, it does happen!). You need to be responsible about your borrowing. Keep in mind that you may not make a whole lot of money after you graduate from college, so be responsible with your borrowing – in fact, avoid borrowing if you can help it! Hefty paychecks could take years of working in your career to arrive, if they ever come at all.

If you are wondering what your occupation pays, the U.S. Department of Labor Bureau of Labor Statistics offers wages that are defined by occupation and area. Although the site does not include starting salaries, it does give you a sense of what you will earn in your occupation. You can find out more at: **www.bls.gov**.

The Credit Card Trap

Those little plastic cards look so innocent, but they can sure get you in a lot of trouble. It is easy to forget that all that credit card spending must be paid back with interest. And that interest adds up fast! You could wind up paying twice as much for your purchase if you have a credit card with high interest that you do not pay off every month. Plus, add in late fees, overlimit fees, and you could pay three times as much for the item as it cost in the first place. Let us look at the credit card trap in greater detail.

Why does a credit card wind up costing you so much more than if you would have made your purchase in cash?

- Some interest rates reach higher than 22 percent. You may find low-rate cards, but often the low rate is an introductory rate, so it is short-lived.

- Penalty interest rates are typically 30 percent, up to as much as 40 percent.

- Late fees are often $39 a month. And you do not have 30 days to get your payment in on time.

- Overlimit fees are typically $35. Are you wondering why you can go over your limit? The credit card companies make money off you doing so.

- Credit card companies can increase your interest rate if you are late with your payments. All of a sudden you interest rate will jump, and if you do not pay close attention, you might not even notice that it did. You should check your statement every month to see if the rate increased. If so, find a new card!

Those are many fees that could really cost you if you do not stay on top of paying your bill on time, staying within your limit, and shopping around for a low-interest card. in business by charging users these hefty fees.

So what do you do if you have racked up credit cards?

- **Don't start using them in the first place:** You are probably spending way more than you need to. When you use a credit card you are paying entirely too much for your purchase in the long run, once you add up the fees.

- **Try to pay off the entire amount every month.**

- **If you must have a credit card, have as few as possible:** Most of us do need one to make purchases on the internet, or to place a purchase on hold, but one or two should suffice.

- **Pay more than the minimum payment:** If you cannot pay the entire amount, pay more than the minimum payment; you will save on interest in the long run.

- **Do not be late with your payments:** Credit card companies often do not give you a full 30 days to make your payment. As soon as you get the bill, check the payment due date. Make sure you send payment seven to 10 days ahead of the due date, so it arrives in time.

- **Ask for help from your credit card company:** If you owe a lot of money on credit cards and cannot seem to make even your minimum payments, try to ask your credit card company for help. They may work with you and give you a lower interest rate or reduce your payment. You can also request to change the due date for another time during the month when it's easier for you to pay.

- **Try transferring your balance to a lower interest credit card:** Some cards offer single-digit interest rates, or even zero percent for a certain amount of time. It may make sense to find a new card again when the introductory rate runs out.

Scholarship and Aid Scams

Let's talk about scholarship scams. Since it is such an enormous and expensive issue for consumers, it is worthwhile to spend some time going over possible scams in detail. There are plenty of ways to scam people, and scholarships, grants, and loan companies are no exception in looking for a way to bilk you out of your money or personal information.

Here are a few things to keep in mind when applying for any type of college funding or loans:

- **Do not give money away to get money:** You should not have to pay someone to find you free money. It is not free money if you have to pay someone to get it for you. Besides, you can do your own research for finding scholarships, grants, and loans for free.

- **There are no guarantees:** No one can guarantee that you will receive a scholarship, grant, or loan.

- **Be careful about giving out your identity and personal information:** Unless you are working with a reputable source such as **www.fafsa.ed.gov**, be careful of giving out your personal information, such as your Social Security number or bank and credit card information. Identity theft occurs often.

- **Watch out for tactics:** "Hurry" or "rush" are scare tactics to try to get you to cave in and act now. Do not trust anyone who uses these measures.

- **Read all documents carefully:** Do not forget to read the fine print. That is where the tricks are often buried.

- **Make sure that you are dealing with a legitimate business:** If you have doubts, do research. Call the Better Business Bureau. Listen to your hunches. If it sounds too good to be true, it probably is.

To contact the Better Business Bureau:

The Council of Better Business Bureaus
4200 Wilson Blvd, Suite 800
Arlington, VA 22203-1838
www.bbb.org

For more information on what to watch out for with scams, visit the FTC at **www.ftc.gov/scholarshipscams**.

Finaid.com offers helpful information about **www.finaid.org/scholar ships/scams.phtml**.

Report financial aid fraud

A company charging for financial aid advice is committing fraud if it does not deliver what it promises. For more information about financial aid fraud, or to report fraud, call the Federal Trade Commission toll free at 877-FTC-HELP or 877-382-4357, or go to **www.ftc.gov/ scholarshipscams**.

Report identity theft

If you suspect that your student information has been stolen, it is important to act quickly. These offices will help you determine what steps to take depending on your situation:

> **U.S. Department of Education**
> **Office of Inspector General Hotline**
> **800-MIS-USED (1-800-647-8733)**
> **Federal Trade Commission**
> **877-IDTHEFT (1-877-438-4338)**

Scholarship Search Scams

Scholarship search scams are a category of scams. What they do is make you pay to have them conduct searches for scholarships that you can conduct yourself for free.

According to the FTC, scam artists advertise in free campus newspapers, flyers, post cards, and on the internet, and charge from $10 to over $1,000 for their services. According to the FTC, however, students who rely on a fraudulent search service instead of doing their own homework when applying for scholarships or grants will face the upcoming school year bills with nothing for the effort but a hard-earned lesson.

Charging for these services is not illegal, but all they are doing is providing you with information that you can obtain for free from reputable sources. No scholarship search company has information that you cannot find out on your own for free, using sources like **www.fastweb.com**.

What to watch out for with scholarship search scams:

- **Secret scholarships:** As mentioned above, there are never any scholarships that are secret or have secret information. Anyone taking some time and effort to find out about scholarships may do so.

- **Guarantees:** A scholarship search company cannot guarantee that you will get a scholarship even if they find one for you.

- **Forcing you to make purchases:** You should not have to make a purchase to have a shot at winning a scholarship. Neither should you be subject to a plethora of pop-up windows and banners trying to entice you to spend your money.

- **Fake scholarships:** Some scholarships themselves are not even legitimate. They are pretending to be scholarships in the effort to get your money or personal information and try to charge you fees to apply.

Remember to keep your personal information safe. Do not give out your Social Security number, your banking information, your PIN number, or any other information to any source that is not verified as a legitimate business.

If you are dealing with a company that you suspect is scamming you, document everything. Get it all in writing, and report the company as soon as possible.

Dropping Courses

Sometimes, whether you want to or not, you are faced with having to drop a class. Maybe you got too busy with work or other classes, or perhaps you are feeling burned out and you want a break. Or you decide that you hate the class that you enrolled in, took too heavy a courseload, or that the class is just too difficult for you now. There are many reasons why students drop classes. Dropping a class may be your best bet in some situations, if you do not think you could pass the class or you changed your mind on your course of study, provided that is it is early in the semester and you can still get a refund.

It is always in your best interest to know the last drop/add date for the semester, or you could wind up with an F or a W (withdrawal). But even if you can get a refund, you may still be at a loss by dropping a class.

Some schools may only give you a partial refund for dropping a class, unless it is in the first week or so. But even then, you may still be stuck with losing money on school fees, books, and other expenses that you invested for the class.

Something else to consider before you fill out that drop slip is that by dropping a class, you may be holding down fewer credits than are allowed in order to receive funding, insurance, or other benefits. For instance, your health insurance or car insurance may be offering you special rates if you are a full-time student. Drop a class or two and you might lose out on your full-time student discounts.

You also need to find out if your grants, loans, or scholarships require that you maintain a certain number of credits per semester. You could potentially lose that money if you drop a class.

When thinking about dropping a class, you should also consider graduation. Is losing this class going to throw off your graduation date? Is it a required class, meaning you will have to take it and get it over with at some point? Is it a prerequisite for other courses so that dropping it is going to mess up your next few semesters' schedule?

If you are having trouble with a class, you could speak with your professor about how to make the class go more smoothly. Perhaps you can get a pass/fail grade instead of a letter grade, or ask about an incomplete. You could speak with your adviser and find out about tutoring. Sometimes you may find that the best option is sticking it out and finishing the class.

Dropping Out

It is unfortunate but true that many college students do not finish their degrees.

Some students cannot handle the academic rigors. Some realize that they cannot afford college. Others wind up in life-changing situations that make college impossible. No matter what obstacles you come across, though, it is a good idea to try to finish. Generally, those who earn degrees make more than those without them. Plus, if you drop out of school, you may have to pay money that was given to you as a scholarship or grant.

When you think about the cost of dropping out of school, you might want to consider trying to find a way to work on your degree, even if it means only taking a few classes at a time over a longer time period.

You could consider night school, online schools, or extension classes. You can find plenty of accredited degrees from many schools that offer these alternative means of getting your degree.

Before you drop out of school, always speak with your academic adviser. He or she may have some good insights or ideas that can help you figure out a way to make staying in school work.

Bankruptcy and Default

Student loans cannot be discharged through bankruptcy. A qualifying education loan is a loan made specifically to pay the higher education expenses of a student who is either the borrower or dependent of the borrower and is enrolled at least half-time at a school.

Where to Go for Help

If you need payment arrangements, are in danger of delinquency, believe that a payment has not been accurately recorded, or have a question about your loan, contact your lender or loan servicer. The person who first answers the phone may not be knowledgeable enough to give an answer about a complicated situation; explain your situation fully, and enlist his or her help in finding the right person to speak to.

While you are in school, or if you plan to return to school, you can get counseling and assistance from the school's financial aid department.

The Office of Federal Student Aid Ombudsman was created by the Department of Education in 1998 to resolve disputes concerning student loans. The Ombudsman will informally investigate complaints from a neutral, independent viewpoint and recommend solutions. The Ombudsman website can be found at **www.ombudsman.ed.gov/** and has numerous resources that can answer your questions and help you resolve your own problems.

The National Consumer Law Center's Student Borrower Assistance Program, at **www.studentloanborrowerassistance.org**, offers step-by-step guidance for solving student loan problems, and answers a variety of questions.

Wrapping It Up

Just as important to finding great deals and free money for college is staying on top of the money you have and avoiding getting scammed. Keep your eyes open and your wallet and personal information close to you. If you suspect a scam, document everything and make sure you report the scam to officials.

If you are thinking about dropping a class or dropping out of school, keep in mind what you may run into financially. Dropping a class may cost you more than you expected. Think hard before making decisions about your school. Speak with your adviser about the implications of your school decisions -- he or she may have the right advice to help you make the right decision.

Conclusion

ow, I know what you might be thinking – that's a lot of work to remain debt-free and get a college degree! Don't lose hope. Everything worthwhile in life requires hard work, but it ultimately makes your life better.

Remember some tips to succeed in college:

- Nobody will care about your degree more than you. If you want it, then put in the hard work to finish. You will make more money with a degree than without – so consider that!

- If you must take out a loan, make extra payments. If you budget for one loan payment every four weeks instead of every month, you will end up making 13 payments in a year instead of 12.

- Work hard to keep up your GPA. Your grades, GPA, and SAT and ACT scores all dictate how much scholarship money you will receive. Committees look at these scores to decide how well-rounded and hard-working a student is, and give them money based on these numbers. While a person isn't strictly a number, on paper this is all a committee can see. Keep your paper-image looking good, and reap the rewards of working hard on your grades.

- Consider a career in law-enforcement, teaching, or any government-paid position that offers student loan forgiveness.

- Remember, a quick online search can help you find cheap places to purchase textbooks. Renting or buying textbooks anywhere but the college bookstore can save you *thousands* of dollars over the course of your education. Check places like **Chegg.com, Textbooks.com, Amazon.com** for cheap books! Be aware that one-time-use access codes can't be purchased as a rental since most of the time they've already been used.

- Try to lower your interest rate! High interest makes a student loan unbearable, so take advantage of all available discounts or consolidation techniques. Once your interest rate is low enough, pay it off as quickly as possible. Be free of major debt! Walk across your graduation stage with not even a penny of debt to your name!

- Make a budget *and stick to it.* I've made plenty of budgets before – which are easy to do with new apps coming out every day – but sticking to them has never been my strong suit. I managed to leave college with no debt to my name by working part-time, taking a full load of classes, and using financial aid and scholarships as much as possible. Living within my means even allowed me to buy my first home at age 20. If I can do it, you can too!

- Dedicate extra income to your college fund. If you receive a graduation gift or even income from a second job, *put it toward your college tuition!* You will save money by paying off your loan early, and when it is paid off, you will be free to devote your money to other purposes. Remember, sticking to a budget now might not seem fun when your friends go out for an evening on the town or take a trip to a theme park, but you'll be walking away debt-free. There's always time after college to take a trip to Europe with the money you saved during college – and it'll be that much sweeter with no debt to your name!

When you think about being able to write your educational background on your resume – B.A., MA., Ph.D. – as well as increasing your chances of being promoted in your job, and making more money than if you did not have a degree, and being happier and perhaps healthier, all the number crunching and strict budgeting will have been worth it. You will be glad you finished your degree, and walked away debt-free!

Appendices

Appendix A

Creating a repayment plan

Step 1: Student loan summary

Gather all your student loan documents and fill in the chart below. When you have finished, total up the outstanding loan balance and the total monthly payments. You can print out and fill in the worksheet from FinAid.org if you prefer (**www.finaid.org/ loans/studentloan-checklist.phtml**).

Student Loan Summary

SCHOOL AND TYPE OF LOAN	LOAN #1	LOAN #2	LOAN #3	LOAN #4	LOAN #5
Loan Servicer and Contact Info					
URL, Log in and Password					
Origination Date					
End Date					
Amount of Loan					
Principal Outstanding (Date)					
Interest Outstanding (Date)					
Interest					
Interest Rate					
Status					
Entered Repayment					
Monthly Payment Amount					
Date Due Every Month					
Interest - Repayment 10 Years					
TOTAL					

Step 2: Debt obligations

List all your debt obligations, including mortgage, auto loans, and credit card debt on the chart below. In the first row, put the total from your student loan chart:

Debt Obligations					
COMPANY	ACCT NO.	BALANCE	APR	MINIMUM MONTHLY PAYMENT	MONTHS TO PAY OFF
Student Loans					
TOTAL					

Step 3: Income

List all your regular monthly income from all sources. If your income is irregular, list your income over a period of several months, and divide by the number of months.

Income Summary	
SOURCE	**AMOUNT**
TOTAL	

Step 4: Debt-to-income ratio

Take your total monthly debt from Step 2, and divide it by your total income from Step 3. This will give you your debt-to-in-come ratio.

Step 5: Adjust your payments

If your debt-to-income ratio exceeds 21 percent, you are overextending yourself and will need to be careful. If it exceeds 36 percent, you are in financial danger and need to take action to reduce the size of your loan payments, such as switching to an extended or income-based repayment plan or asking for forbearance or de- ferment until you can increase your income.

Are your circumstances only temporary? Are you looking for employ-ment, or do you expect your income to increase when you start a new job next month? If so, live frugally for the present, and revisit your debt-to-income ratio in two or three months.

Are you expecting a windfall, such as a tax refund or a resettlement allowance from the Peace Corps? Use it to pay down your student loan balance, which will lower your monthly payment, or to eliminate credit card debt or another debt obligation.

Step 6: Create a budget

Gather your bank statements, credit card statements, and cash receipts and write down your monthly living expenses. You may be able to do this quickly using online banking.

Subtract your debt obligations from Step 2 from your total income in Step 3 to see how much you have available for living expenses. Decide how much of your monthly income should be allocated to each spending category, and stick to your budget. Budget-tracking software can help you monitor your spending and stay on track.

Step 7: Look for extra money

Examine your budget for areas where you could reduce your spending, and find extra money to pay your debt obligations faster. See Chapter 15. Postpone a major purchase, such as a car, appliance, or vacation, and pay down your loan balance or credit card debt instead. Increase the amount going into your savings, and when it surpasses a specified amount, use the extra to pay off your debts. Sell something of value that you do not need anymore. Look for ways to earn extra income.

Step 8: Establish a pattern that will increase your prosperity

Make freedom from debt a priority. Develop a strategy for steadily paying off your student loans and other debt obligations while putting aside savings for emergencies and future expenses. Manage your loans and other debts efficiently so that your credit score improves and you can get lower interest rates. Periodically review your credit reports and refinance your debt when your credit score improves. Save up for a down payment on a house, car, or boat.

Appendix B

The following websites may be helpful in your quest to find cash for school. The websites were mentioned in the book, but here they are again for your reference. There are also plenty more out there!

- www.1800goguard.com
- www.amazon.com
- www.amazon.co.uk
- apps.collegeboard.com/fincalc/sla.jsp

- www.bigwords.com
- www.bls.gov
- www.campusbooks.com
- www.dl.ed.gov/borrower/DefermentFormList.do?cmd=initializeContext
- www.ebay.com
- www.ed.gov
- www.fafsa.ed.gov
- www.fastweb.com
- www.finaid.org/calculators
- www.finaid.org/calculators/scripts/loanpayments.cgi
- www.finaid.org/scholarships/scams.phtml
- www.floridastudentfinancialaid.org
- www.ftc.gov/scholarshipscams
- www.grants.gov
- www.iCollegeWeb.com
- www.nationalservice.gov/programs/americorps
- www.ombudsman.ed.gov/
- www.Salliemae.com
- www.studentloanborrowerassistance.org
- www.textbooks.com

Appendix C

Budget Worksheet for College Students

INCOME:	Daily	Monthly	Semesterly	Yearly
From Jobs (after taxes)				
From Parents / Family				
From Financial Aid				
Miscellaneous Income				
Other				
Total Income:				

FIXED EXPENSES:	Daily	Monthly	Semesterly	Yearly
Rent / Housing				
Food / Meal Plan				
Car Payment				
Car Insurance & Registration				
Tuition & Fees				
Loan / Credit Card Payments				
Telephone / Cell Phone				
Utilities				
Other				
Total Fixed Expenses:				

FLEXIBLE EXPENSES:	Daily	Monthly	Semesterly	Yearly
Eating Out				
Clothing				
Books				
Entertainment				
Public Transportation				
Cable				
Internet Access				
Personal Hygiene Items (Shampoo, deodorant, etc.)				
Recreation				
Miscellaneous				
Gym				
Child Care				
Laundry / Dry Cleaning				
Travel				
Savings				
Other				
Total Flexible Expenses:				

	Daily	Monthly	Semesterly	Yearly
Total Income:				
Total Fixed Expenses:				
Total Flexible Expenses:				
Balance:				

Glossary

Academic year: A one-year period, often from July 1 to June 30 of the next calendar year. A school that uses terms instead of semesters may count 30 weeks of instructional time as an academic year.

Accrued Interest: Interest that accumulates on the unpaid principal balance of a loan; the amount of money that is repaid on a loan in addition to the original interest.

ACT Assessment: A national college admission examination that consists of tests in English, mathematics, reading, science, and writing.

Adjusted Gross Income (AGI): Taxable income from all sources, calculated on the annual IRS tax return.

Advanced Placement (AP) Courses: College-level classes taken by students while they are still in high school.

AmeriCorps: A U.S. national service program that gives education credits in exchange for a year of public service.

Balance: The amount that remains to be repaid on a loan.

Bankruptcy: A legal declaration that an individual is unable to pay his or her debts, usually resulting in debt relief.

Consolidation loan: A single loan taken out to pay off multiple loans at a more favorable interest rate.

Cost of Attendance: The estimated cost, as determined by a school, of attendance for one year, including tuition, fees, room and board, books, supplies, and incidental expenses.

Credit score: A numerical assessment of an individual's ability to repay a loan.

Default: Failure to repay a loan.

Deferment: A temporary suspension of a loan payments granted to borrowers in specific circumstances.

Department of Education: The U.S. government agency that administers the student financial aid and loan program.

Direct Loan: A subsidized or unsubsidized federal loan administered directly through the school.

Discharge: The cancellation of all principal and interest owed on a loan.

DOE: The U.S. Department of Education.

Exit Counseling: Education about loan repayment offered to a borrower at the time of leaving school.

Expected Family Contribution (EFC): A calculation of how much a student and the student's family are expected to pay out of pocket for an education.

Extended Repayment Plan: A repayment plan that lowers the amount of each monthly payment by extending the term of the loan.

FAFSA: Free Application for Federal Student Aid.

Federal Direct Consolidation Loan: A Direct Loan that refinances several individual government loans as a single loan with a lower interest rate.

Federal Family Education Loans (FFEL): A program in which loans are made by private lenders and subsidized and guaranteed by the federal government.

Forbearance: An agreement in which a lender allows a borrower to temporarily delay or reduce payments during a period of financial hardship.

Grant: Money given to a student to pay for education-related expenses.

Guarantor: A third party that guarantees to pay a lender the outstanding principal and interest of a student loan if the borrower defaults on the loan.

Health Resources and Services Administration (HRSA): A federal government agency that administers student loans for future health service workers.

Interest capitalization cap: A limit placed on the amount of unpaid interest that can be capitalized (added to the loan balance).

Lender: A bank or institution that provides the funds for a student loan and receives the interest.

Loan forgiveness program: Program that forgives federal student loans for borrowers employed in specific occupations.

Loans for Disadvantaged Students: A program for long-term, low-interest loans for full-time students earning a degree in allopathic medicine, osteopathic medicine, dentistry, optometry, podiatric medicine, pharmacy, or veterinary medicine.

Military Deferment: A deferment given to members of the Armed Forces who are deployed on active duty during a war or national emergency.

Nursing Student Loan Program: A program that provides long-term, low-interest rate loans to full-time and half-time students of nursing.

Pell Grant: A need-based federal grant to pay qualified education expenses.

Perkins Loans: Low-interest subsidized loans awarded by a school to undergraduate and graduate students with exceptional financial need.

PIN: Department of Educational Personal Identification Number. A four-digit confidential ID number used to electronically sign the FAFSA and access personal loan information online.

PLUS Loans: Parental Loan for Undergraduate Studies loans.

Primary Care Loan (PCL): A program that offers low cost federal loans for medical students who commit themselves to entering primary health care practice for a minimum period of time.

Prepaid College Tuition plan: A savings plan that allows families to lock in the current cost of tuition at a university by paying it in advance.

Principal: The original amount of a loan.

Rehabilitation: The procedure for bringing a loan out of default and reinstituting a payment plan.

Sallie Mae: A student loan company created as a government enterprise in 1972 to administer federally-insured loans, and privatized in 2004.

Scholarship: Money given to a student to pay for education.

Student Aid Report (SAR): A report of a student's eligibility for financial aid, prepared by the Department of Education.

Standard Repayment Plan: A student loan repayment plan under which you make a fixed monthly payment for a term of up to ten years.

Subsidized student loan: A Stafford loan for which the government pays the interest while the student is in school and during periods of deferment.

Title IV: The portion of the Higher Education Act of 1965 that provides for the administration of federal student financial aid.

Unsubsidized student loan: A Stafford loan for which interest accrues during the time the student is in school and during deferment periods.

Bibliography

"AmeriCorps." *Corporation for National and Community Service.*
Corporation for National and Community Service, n.d. Web.
11 July 2017.

"An Introduction to 529 Plans." *SEC Emblem.*
U.S. Securities And Exchange Commission, 08 Aug. 2012. Web.

"Chick and Sophie Major Memorial Duck Calling Contest."
Scholarships for College Free College Scholarship. Scholarships,
n.d. Web. 5 June 2017. **(https://www.scholarships.com/financial-aid/
college-scholarships/scholarships-by-type/unusual-scholarships/
chick-and-sophie-major-memorial-duck-calling-contest/)**

CollegeBoard. Trends in College Pricing 2008. Trends in Higher Education Series. College Board, 2008. **(http://professionals. collegeboard.com/profdownload/trends-in-student-aid-2008.pdf)** Accessed 2 July 2017.

"Coverdell Education Savings Account (ESA)." Publication 970 (2016), Tax Benefits for Education. Internal Revenue Service, 2016. Web. 18 July 2017. **(https://www.irs.gov/publications/p970/ch07.html)**

"Fees and Fee Reductions." AP Exam Fees and Reductions. College Board, 2017. Web. 18 July 2017. **(https://apstudent.collegeboard.org/takingtheexam/exam-fees)**.

"Frequently Asked Questions." *Corporation for National and Community Service.* N.p., n.d. Web. 05 July 2017.

"Get Started." Get Started – CLEP – The College Board. College Board, 2017. Web. 18 July 2017. **<https://clep.collegeboard.org/earn-college-credit/get-started>**.

Kirkham, Elyssa. "Study: Here's the Real Cost Per Credit Hour Students Have to Pay." Student Loan Hero. N.p., 21 Feb. 2017. Web. 18 July 2017. **(https://studentloanhero.com/featured/ cost-per-credit-hour-study/)**

"Lambert and Annetje Van Valckenburg Memorial Scholarship." *National Association of the Van Valckenburg(h) Family Scholarship Fund.* The National Association of the Van Valckenburg Family, n.d. Web. 17 June 2017. **(http://navvf.org/scholarship.html)**

"Our World-Underwater Society Rolex Scholarship." *Scholarships for College Free College Scholarship*. Scholarships, n.d. Web. 10 June 2017. **(http://www.scholarships.com/financial-aid/ college-scholarships/scholarships-by-type/weird-scholarships/ our-world-underwater-society-rolex-scholarships/)**

"Public Service Loan Forgiveness." *Federal Student Aid*. Office of the U.S. Department of Education, 01 June 2017. Web. 11 July 2017. **(http://studentaid.ed.gov/sa/repay-loans/forgiveness-cancellation/ public-service)**

"Stafford Loan Frequently Asked Questions." *US News*. U.S. News & World Report L.P., 17 Aug. 2010. Web. 17 June 2017. **(http://www.usnews.com/education/best-colleges/ paying-for-college/student-loan/articles/2010/08/17/ stafford-loan-frequently-asked-questions)**

U.S. Department of Education, National Center for Education Statistics. (2016). *Digest of Education Statistics, 2015* (NCES 2016-014), Chapter 3.

"U.S. Student Loan Debt Statistics for 2017." *Student Loan Hero*. N.p., 17 May 2017. Web. 11 July 2017. **http://studentloanhero.com/ student-loan-debt-statistics**

Bidwell, Allie. "Student Loan Expectations: Myth vs. Reality." *U.S. News & World Report*. U.S. News & World Report, 07 Oct. 2014. Web. 17 July 2017.

"Public Service Loan Forgiveness." *Federal Student Aid*. U.S. Department of Education, 01 June 2017. Web. 17 July 2017.

Index

About the Author

icole DeIorio is a native Floridian, and received her degree at the University of Central Florida in English - Creative Writing. Ever since she was a little girl, storytelling and writing have captured her heart. First putting pen to paper at the age of twelve, Nicole has written numerous short stories, poems, and scripts. Her goals include publishing one of the fantasy books she's writing, and owning a magazine company one day. When she's not writing, she enjoys practicing Krav Maga, working out at her local CrossFit gym, and traveling across the United States. She aspires to run a half-marathon and take part in her first CrossFit competition within the next year. She's interned for Ocala Magazine, where she wrote over a dozen articles.

Photo by Chris Redd Photography